POLISH-BORN NELLY BEN-OR is a distinguished pianist and teacher. She has recorded a variety of recital programmes for the BBC, performed in London at the major venues, as well as throughout the UK and in many countries overseas. In 1963 she qualified as a teacher of the Alexander Technique – the first professional pianist to become so. This made a significant impact on her approach to piano playing and music-making in general. She is now recognised internationally as an outstanding exponent of the application of principles of the Alexander Technique to various fields of music-making, especially piano playing. She is in great demand to share this approach, which she does through master classes at music conservatoires, university music departments, and through her own twice-yearly international courses for pianists in London. Since 1975 she has been on the teaching staff of the keyboard department at London's Guildhall School of Music and Drama.

'An inspiring story, beautifully written, that tells of a young Jewish girl's survival in Nazi-occupied Poland, hidden by a series of righteous Christians who risked their lives by their actions, supported by a wealthy Uncle (also living a hidden life) and above all by the indomitable spirit and faith of the author and her mother. In hiding, the dream of Nelly Ben-Or was to become a concert pianist and after liberation we see her make this dream a reality, helped by her discovery of the Alexander Technique and, again, good people entering her life at the right times.'

– Rabbi Dr Andrew Goldstein,
President, Liberal Judaism

'This is a brilliant and deeply moving personal account. Nelly Ben-Or's retelling of a story, so familiar to us, is written through her own childhood's eyes in words of such poignant simplicity that they sing to us across the clamour of the intervening years. One cannot help but be moved to tears.'

Jonathan Vaughan, Vice Principal and
Director of Music, Guildhall School of Music & Drama

'A role model for pianists with the ring of the legendary, Nelly Ben-Or's now-famous pioneer work in adapting the Alexander Technique for pianists has made a major contribution to pedagogy for well over half a century. Her gripping autobiography tells the tale of personal struggle and achievement against the harrowing background of survival of the Lwów ghetto and Warsaw Uprising, musical education in post-war Poland and the nascent State of Israel, as well as her increasingly international ambit since settling in Britain in the 1960s. The eminently readable book is both historical and personal testimony, narrating her spiritual journey with enriching, introspective detail. Like her recitals, masterclasses, and summer courses, it promises to inspire pianists, musicians, scholars, as well as all those interested in the triumph of the human spirit over adversity.'

Dr Malcolm Miller Hon Associate, the Open University and
Editor of *Arietta: Journal of the Beethoven Piano Society of Europe*

Ashes to Light

A HOLOCAUST CHILDHOOD
TO A LIFE IN MUSIC

NELLY BEN-OR

I.B. TAURIS

LONDON · NEW YORK

Published in 2018 by
I.B.Tauris & Co. Ltd
London • New York
www.ibtauris.com

ISBN: 978 1 78831 309 4
eISBN: 978 1 78672 381 9
ePDF: 978 1 78673 381 8

A full CIP record for this book is available from the British Library
A full CIP record is available from the Library of Congress

Library of Congress Catalog Card Number: available

Typeset by Initial Typesetting Services, Edinburgh
Printed and bound in Litauen by ScandBook UAB

To the memory of my parents:
my father, brutally murdered by the Nazis,
and my mother, whose love and courage enabled
me to survive the terrors of the Holocaust.

Contents

List of Illustrations

All images courtesy of the author unless otherwise stated

1. Grandfather Isidor Linden – Mother's father
2. Grandmother Leah Helen Linden – Mother's mother
3. Nelly aged 4 with her parents and sister on holiday before the war
4. L-R, Mother, Nelly and Alicja Topolska in Warsaw during the war
5. Nelly with Zygmunt Topolski and, on the left, Alicja and Mrs Topolska, Mother and Jola in Warsaw during the war
6. The destruction of Warsaw during World War II (*Public domain*)
7. Sister Janette, in 1946
8. Mother, in 1946
9. Nelly with her sister and mother shortly after the end of the war
10. Janette and her husband Julian
11. Nelly at the Mozart Piano Competition, Israel 1952

Preface

From the first years of my coming to England, in 1960, I was repeatedly asked to tell the story of my childhood experiences under the Nazi occupation of Poland between the years 1939 and 1945. I gave talks to various groups and societies of mostly, though not only, Jewish people; many of them knew something about those dark times from what they had read or heard about from relatives who had come to England during or after the war, fortunate to have escaped or, even luckier, to have survived the Holocaust despite the dangers and threats of annihilation. On such occasions I was usually asked whether I had written about my experiences, which eventually led to my deciding to do so.

The first part of this narrative, describing my childhood years during World War II, was written very slowly. I made a solemn promise to myself that, once I started to write, there would be no interruption in continuing the account. I committed myself to writing at least one page in long hand every day, regardless of circumstances, even if it meant that sometimes I could only do so in the late hours of the night. I felt the need to fulfil this commitment and complete writing the full story of my living through the Holocaust.

This, however, took its toll. Having finished the narrative, I fell seriously ill. Remembering and reliving those years of my childhood, imbued with the constant fear of being put to death, brought about a reaction through illness which took some time to recover from. Only years later did I begin also to describe events and influences in my life from the end of the war onwards. This forms the second, third and fourth parts of the book.

The four parts of the narrative are woven together by one central strand which gradually develops: that is, my life with and in music. The strength of my passion for music has seen me through much of my life's journey. So also, did encounters with very special individuals who greatly enriched that journey.

All the events and situations described here are authentic. None of the people or happenings are fictional. My intention was to record the story of my life without added embellishments.

Acknowledgements

I wish to acknowledge my debt of gratitude for the guidance I received over the years from my teachers and mentors: the pianist Henrietta Michaelson and the master teacher of the Alexander Technique, Patrick Macdonald, as well as other people whose special help I benefited from at significant moments in my life: the psychotherapists Dr Schossberger and Peter Hildebrand; Rina Hands who for many years was my spiritual guide through the teachings of G.I. Gurdjieff.

I extend my thanks to Cecily Fernbank for generously making the first typed copy of the Holocaust part of the book from my handwritten script and to Neil Frais for printing a number of copies of it for my use.

The psychologist and therapist George Frankl who, having read one of the copies suggested I should continue the narrative of my life through the post-war years to the present time. This gave me the impetus to do so.

My husband, Roger Clynes, who gave unstintingly of his time and energy in making a first edit of the text, and encouraging me to persevere towards the completion of this memoir.

Our daughter, Daniela, for various comments and suggestions; and the photographer Tony Day for his professional assistance in preparing many of the photographs for publication.

Valery Rees who, on reading the whole manuscript, recommended me to her publisher I.B. Tauris.

Joanna Godfrey, senior editor at I.B. Tauris, for her tireless guidance and assistance in bringing the publication to fruition.

Part I

THE WAR YEARS

CHAPTER 1

1 September 1939 –
Nazis Invade Poland

Friday afternoon – Mother in the midst of Sabbath preparations. There are smells of baking challah, chicken soup simmering and gefilte fish cooking in a dish. The usual Friday afternoon activities in readiness for the Eve of Sabbath. Then suddenly – noise, confusion, explosions of bombs, an unexpected feeling of anxiety; people rushing out of their homes bewildered, asking each other what is happening? The news spreads like an icy wind – war; Hitler has attacked Poland. These are Nazi aeroplanes dropping bombs on the city.

Those were the first moments of what was to turn into more than five years of darkness. The warmth and security of a Jewish home, the closeness of the family, was soon to be shattered. Fear, anxiety, loss and pain were to become the predominant experiences in our lives. And the shadow of violent, cruel, inhuman death was to be cast over our daily experience and enter the depths of our disturbed dreams.

I was a little girl, just six years old. Our home was a small apartment in Królowej Jadwigi – one of the quieter central streets of the Polish city of Lwów (also formerly known as Lemberg, its German name; it is now called Lviv, and is in the Ukraine). There was my parents' bedroom with a balcony overlooking the street, the adjoining room with a couch for my sister and a small bed for me, and a large kitchen-living room with a partitioned part containing the cooking area. The sliding doors of the partition were a tempting attraction to play with. The apartment building had an inner courtyard with a balcony running outside the kitchen door. It was on that balcony that I later stood pressed in fear against my mother's skirt watching the Nazis carry out all the lovely belongings of our home. I remember them taking away the piano.

My only sister Fryderyka, or 'Frydzia' as she was called, was about 14. Mother and Father, who were in their thirties, kept a traditional Jewish home. A young Ukrainian peasant girl lived with us to help with some of the housework.

Mother must have been very pretty with dark brown eyes, black hair and a well-shaped face. She devoted all her time to looking after us and to her own creative way of running our home. Mother was most gifted and creative in all manner of embroidery, knitting and crochet work. Almost all of the clothes worn by Frydzia and me were handmade and hand-embroidered. I can remember dresses, blouses, petticoats, all made in a variety of styles and patterns of embroidery. There were sweaters, shawls, muffs, gloves, hats and socks: all Mother's own exquisitely expert work. One could tell the difference in quality and finesse of workmanship between the things she made for us and those ready-made, which others wore. This was but a small part of the output of her creativity. Our modest apartment was decorated with Mother's handcrafted items, the products of endless hours of her work. There was not a single window curtain that was not adorned by Mother's own embroidery, lace or fringe; not a bed, nor sofa, covered in anything but spreads of beautiful fabric decorated by her embroidery, petit-points, or appliqué work. The same was true of all our tablecloths, napkins, pillow cases and sheets. Mother also produced small- and large-scale picture embroidery as wall hangings, or framed pictures. In our living room hung one of Mother's finest and largest tapestries – a most colourfully embroidered picture of Little Red Riding Hood carrying her basket through the woods. This one seemed to please Mother most and she enjoyed showing it as one of her best works. It hung over the object of special significance and affection in our family – the piano. That is one of my first memories of the instrument which was later to become so central in my life.

My father is a much more elusive figure in my memory. He travelled much as a sales representative of a large firm called Hardtmuth, which manufactured fine fountain pens and pencils. A fountain pen was to me, then, a symbol of adulthood. Children used crayons, and only later learned to write properly with pen and ink. Father used to come home for the Sabbath arriving on Friday evenings with special treats for the family. I can remember the delicious taste of halva brought by him, or the special flavour of kosher 'ham'. On my birthday, just a few months before the outbreak of the war, he gave me a beautiful children's edition of *The Odyssey*.

The story of the one-eyed Cyclops left somewhere a lasting impression in my memory.

Ours was a warm, cosy, safe-feeling family. The formal traditions of a Jewish home were kept quite assiduously. We ate kosher food, kept the Sabbath, and celebrated all the Jewish festivals; my parents could read Hebrew prayers – and we went to the synagogue. Friday night, the Eve of Sabbath, was the highlight of the week, with Mother preparing lovely traditional meals and baking her own challah (the plaited Sabbath bread). She lit candles before the meal, and I remember her covering her hair with a scarf and saying a blessing over the candlelight, standing in front of it, hands covering her face. There was a feeling of a special atmosphere of the Holy day in our home. I can remember my father with the prayer shawl over his shoulders, his head covered and wearing the '*tefillim*' (phylacteries) on his forehead, saying his prayers in the corner of the room.

My sister was several years older than me. She was the pretty one of the family, with lovely dark brown eyes and rich black hair. She was very musical, played the piano and had a lovely soprano singing voice. She was lively, intelligent and of a sparkling temperament. As a little girl, I looked up to her as the model of female attractiveness and inevitably wanted to emulate her. She was sent to a Jewish Hebrew-speaking school. It was for my sister that our parents bought a piano, a tremendous luxury for a family with only a modest income. Soon after the instrument was installed in our home I began to be drawn to it, making up harmonies to accompany the songs which my sister sang. Noticing my musicality, she began to give me my first instruction in reading music, which soon led to my being taken to a teacher at the age of about five. I remember the times before we had this magical instrument in our home – I used to arrange a small stool as a 'piano' and sit on a lower one next to it 'playing' imaginary piano music with great abandon. . . !

It was soon obvious that I had a real musical gift and my passion for music – with a special love of the piano – began to manifest itself. I made rapid strides in learning to play. After a short while, the teacher transferred me to a more advanced class and there was talk around me about my gift as a little pianist. It looked as if my vocation had been found and the future was clearly mapped out for me. Piano pieces succeeded one another swiftly. In a youth concert, I played some pieces from Tchaikovsky's 'Album for the Young'. But this was all before 1st September 1939.

That fateful day in my childhood marked the beginning of a period of more than five years of frightening events, great anxiety and with the shadow of death hovering over us all. Suddenly the peaceful flow of our lives was shattered. We began to live in fear, running into cellars to shelter from air raids. This, however, soon turned out to be not the worst compared with what was yet to come. From that day the warm, safe feeling of childhood life was destroyed and a succession of frightening, inexplicable experiences followed one another. Life turned into endless stretches of threatening situations. There was the fear and threat of fighting going on around us and hunger, with fewer and fewer food products available. Even that was by no means the worst. Gradually we began to discover that there was something fundamentally 'wrong' with us. We were Jews. This became at first a derogatory word, then a term of persecution and in the end a death sentence.

My father, Leon, was one of two sons of a very orthodox Jewish family. The family name was Podhoretz. His brother was married and had a son and daughter; they must have been of early school age just before the war broke out. My recollection of Father's family is not very detailed and centres mainly around his parents whom I remember as being old and dressed in traditionally orthodox garments with grandmother wearing a *scheitel* (wig), as all orthodox married women did, and grandfather a long black coat and round hat with a large fur rim, underneath which one could see his single hairlock by the side of each cheek. I learned many years after the war that my paternal grandfather was a synagogue cantor, with a very fine voice.

I have much more vivid memories of Mother's family, the Lindens. There were four brothers and three sisters, my mother being the middle one of the sisters. The family seems to have had much talent and lively 'esprit'. They were also extremely good looking and the sons had great charm and liked, and were liked by, ladies. The same was true of their very impressive looking handsome father, my grandfather, Isidor. Life was perhaps rough for my grandmother Leah Helen, who must have gone through some extremely hard times while bringing up her large family, often on slim resources. She was schooled in basic Judaism, could read Hebrew prayers well and was quite observant in her ways but was not as orthodox as my father's parents were. I remember her from my early childhood as being in charge of a large farmhouse in a village where my grandfather looked after a country estate belonging to a Polish landowner.

My mother, speaking in praise of the resilience and strong character of her own mother, used to tell a story which illustrated my grandmother's sharpness of mind. Apparently a woman came to Grandma Helen – 'Babcia' as we called her – to tell her of my grandfather's philandering exploits. She asked Babcia whether she knew that her husband had given a lovely fur coat to the attractive blonde woman in the next village. Without a moment's hesitation or expression of annoyance, Babcia replied 'What a pity you don't look like that blonde or he would have given you a fur coat too!'

Uncle Tadeusz, the youngest son, followed in my grandfather's footsteps. His interests lay in agriculture and he eventually received a degree in agronomy. One brother, Janek, became a bank employee and later in 1944 died with the resistance fighters during the Warsaw Uprising. Another brother went as an apprentice to a watchmaker and jeweller from an early age, and was soon earning well and even helping his parents financially. He was Uncle Max, who became very successful in business and later, during the war, played a most important part in supporting financially (and through that helping to save from annihilation) his own immediate family, my family and a great number of other people who would otherwise have perished under the Nazi occupation. It was Uncle Max whom I remember best from my childhood, partly because he survived the war and also as I have spent time with him on several occasions since then.

The summers of those early years of my life constitute some of my happiest memories. My grandparents' children and grandchildren would go down to their home in a country village in eastern Poland in the vicinity of Lwów, where we all stayed through the summer. Being there, close to nature, living amongst gardens, orchards, domestic and farm animals, was a rich experience for us children as we were used to living in town apartments or houses for most of the year. Those summers of my early childhood have left in me a feeling of yearning for being in the countryside; nostalgia for all we children experienced during those long spells in my grandparents' home: picking huge baskets of cherries, plums, pears, and apples in the orchards, playing in the fields and nearby woods – a setting which gave free rein to our imagination. Some of us, clad in garlands of field flowers and daisy chains, created dramatic presentations of fairy tales. There was magic around us. Memories of the scents, sights and sounds of the countryside in the summer have remained with me always. I remember vividly the violence of occasional spectacular thunderstorms, when we children huddled in corners of the house which seemed so safe to us. That search for safe hiding places was later to assume a terrifying reality.

CHAPTER 2

Beginnings of the Nightmare

Prior to Hitler's conquest of Poland in September 1939, he had concluded a political agreement with Stalin in which they pledged friendship and non-aggression. As part of this pact, the eastern area of Poland, including our city, came under Russian control. There is a Polish saying: '*Z deszczu pod rynne*' which means 'From the rain under the gutter' – in other words, 'Out of the frying pan, into the fire'. Many people began to suffer under the Stalinist regime: they lost their rights, their property and personal freedom. Many were arrested and deported, mostly to Siberia. Anyone who could be even remotely described as part of the aristocracy or bourgeoisie became the victim of Stalin's regime. However Jews, especially if they were not rich or politically influential before the start of the war, were left in relative peace. It was during that time that I began learning a little Russian. There seemed to be relatively little change in my family's way of life then.

However, in 1941, the situation changed with Hitler's offensives against the Russians. Ignoring their pact, Germany

attacked Russia, and pushed the Soviet troops out of eastern Poland, including Lwów. That year, in June, a German
order was issued for the extermination of Jews. Some people
who dreaded the prospect of the Nazis taking over our part
of Poland packed what they could of their personal belongings and began to head further eastwards into Russia. Years
later I heard that my father had suggested to Mother that we
should also join those who were escaping from the on-coming
Germans and follow the retreating Red Army. My mother
looked around at the home she had so devotedly created, the
home which bore so many marks of her talents: the extraordinary embroidery, and all manner of lovely handmade things
on which she had spent endless hours of work. 'How could we
abandon our home and just go on a truck somewhere towards
the unknown?' she said, and refused to leave. I never asked her
later if she regretted that decision, but Father did not survive to
judge whether it had been the right one. Many Jewish people
did in fact survive as refugees in Russia, but the hard labour,
hunger and cold claimed many victims amongst them too.

For those of us who stayed in Poland to experience the
presence of Hitler's Nazis, a state of hell on earth gradually
unfolded. The first act of degradation which the German
occupiers perpetrated was to force all Jewish people, from
the youngest to the oldest, to wear around the arm a white
band with the blue Star of David sewn onto it. This marked
out the Jewish people from the rest of the population and it
made anyone wearing the accursed band an easy target for
abuse and persecution.

Quite soon after the German occupation of eastern
Poland, one of the first things we experienced was the brutal

dispossession of most of our belongings. One day I stood holding on to my mother's skirt as Germans in uniform burst into our home, took everything of value, anything which looked attractive and carted it away as if we had absolutely no right to own what my parents had worked so hard for. I remember a lovely pink porcelain coffee set, all attractive dishes and especially Mother's hand-embroidered wall hangings, tablecloths, bed covers and framed pictures. My mother had spent years of work, denying herself perhaps the pleasure of going out, in order to adorn her nest with her own gifted work. Now it was all suddenly taken away. Finally – the worst thing for me – our piano was removed too. I shivered in fear and despair, huddled against my mother's body as I watched them taking away the instrument which had become for me such a wonderful source of magic. We were left impoverished and degraded, people considered blemished by our Jewish heritage, sub-human, deserving no rights, creatures against whom all insults, cruelty and depravity were apparently justified. The endless succession of humiliating, intimidating and terrifying events had begun.

There were three groups of people amongst the Germans (and not just in Poland): the Wehrmacht were the soldiers of the army, composed of volunteers and conscripts from a range of backgrounds; these were the least frightening. The SS (*Schutzstaffel*) were the highly trained stormtroopers who were engaged in special tasks, such as guarding the Fuhrer and other leading Nazis, rounding up Jews and other 'undesirables' and guarding the concentration and extermination camps. They wore identifying insignia on their uniforms.

The Gestapo were the most feared. They were the so-called 'secret police' and would torture prisoners to gather information about the whereabouts of Jews and resistance fighters, agents and other so-called 'enemies of the state'. They also wore identifying uniforms and insignia.

Later, in November 1941, we were forced to leave our home altogether and move into a very cramped one-room dwelling within the part of the outskirts of the town designated to be the official ghetto for all the Jews of Lwów. There was a high brick wall with broken glass lacing the top of it, together with barbed wire; all this was constructed around the entire ghetto to prevent anyone from escaping. Heavily armed SS men stood guard at different points along the wall. Within the ghetto people from different parts of the city were bundled together, rich and poor, young and old, the most highly educated together with the illiterate ones, Jews who, in pre-war times, hardly knew their Jewish heritage, together with the most strictly orthodox. All of us were thrown into this prison together, to await our impending annihilation. The Nazi 'scientific' mentality and sense of 'practical order' bled every bit of usable energy out of us while we were still alive in the ghetto. All able-bodied and young people were driven in truck-loads, under heavy SS guard, out of the ghetto early each morning to work on projects for the German army: some sewing German uniforms, others working in various other production schemes. Each evening the truck-loads of exhausted, hungry and frightened people would be brought back and 'dumped' in the ghetto for the night, to be picked up again the following dawn. They were the lucky ones – although kept in terror, as long as they could be exploited to do unpaid labour and fed on less than the minimum of the most basic food, they were not immediately exterminated. It is amazing how each person clung to every day of living. Or was it the fear of the kind of end to which our lives were to come that caused us to make such superhuman efforts to cling to life?

My own family – Mother, Father, my sister and I – were cooped up in a small house divided between several families. I remember one room in which we all lived and a corner in a corridor where Mother prepared whatever minimal amounts of food came our way. This was a time of complete deprivation. And it was a time of constant fear of what each day or even hour would bring.

Our existence in the confines of the ghetto was fraught with constant anxiety, which at moments grew into virtually paralysing terror. The Nazis were continually supplying a flow of humans for the concentration camps. The most dreaded of those we heard of were Auschwitz (Oświęcim), Majdanek, Treblinka and Bełżec in Poland. Although I was around eight years of age at the time, I knew these names and overheard frightening conversations in which people were passing on stories that somehow got out of the camps. I knew that no one could remain alive in them. I knew that each inmate was put to death by being taken to a gas chamber. I knew that prior to this horrendous death there was an existence in inhumane conditions with extremely hard labour, almost no food, appalling sanitary conditions, torture and cruelty. Somehow this information got out. Somehow I, a child who in the normal course of life would not have understood even the language describing such things, overheard these conversations and took in all that was spoken of by the frightened adults.

For me, one of the most painful memories from the ghetto days was seeing my father broken down by hunger. I saw him outside our home picking some grass and eating it ravenously. Something snapped in the heart of this little girl. My father's obvious suffering caused something inside me to tighten with pain. I can never recall this scene without re-experiencing that feeling of despair and pity for my father's degradation and helplessness. This must have been my first, most shattering recognition of the vulnerability of that once protecting, reassuring figure who took care of the entire family and had always been the symbol of security. The pain of seeing him in this situation of physical and psychological distress has stayed in my memory over the years.

Every so often, at the most unexpected hours of day or night, a lorry-load of heavily armed SS men would drive into the ghetto, screaming abuse and spreading terror. These men – who were always drunk, possibly to promote better 'performance' of their brutal tasks – would go into 'action' (the name given to these events by the ghetto inmates). An 'action' consisted of dragging as many people as they could find, to be loaded on to their lorries, which were then driven off to special cattle trains. These, with carriages packed full, drove the people to their final destination – the extermination camps.

These 'actions' were the most fearful moments in the ghetto. Sometimes a warning would be given. The word would blow through the neighbourhood like an icy wind that an 'action' had started and we would all scatter in search of hiding places, like hunted animals in their last attempts at saving their lives.

There was a small barn outside the house in which we lived in the ghetto. I remember one night having heard a warning of an approaching lorry full of SS men in 'action'. My family and the other people in the house hid in this barn, all of us squeezed tightly in a small underfloor storage place. We covered the opening as well as possible with old bits of furniture and sat crouched, holding our breath, in this totally dark, damp, small space. The Nazis, not finding anyone in the house, furiously searched the outbuildings. I remember hearing their heavy boots over our heads kicking and pushing about all the scattered objects and bits of broken furniture, yelling in anger ' *Wo sind doch die verfluchten Juden?* ' ('Where are these accursed Jews?'). We were all just under the floor they trampled on, wondering if our last hour had arrived. And then, gradually, we heard the noise of these hunting SS men recede. We could hardly believe that on this occasion they did not guess our hide-out. It was a miracle to us. Had we been found, there would have been the most horrible massacre of us all, on the spot. We stayed for some hours in that hole before daring to go back into our home for some food and drink, and some sleep – hoping for a respite before the next 'hunt', the next 'action'.

During that period, there were many such occasions on which we tried to avoid being taken away and transported to Auschwitz. I remember distinctly one other time when we were hiding with a group of neighbours between the wall of a wooden shed and a fence adjoining it. The space, which was not more than two feet wide and perhaps 12 feet long, was filled with a group of people trying to hide from the approaching, raging SS men who wanted to capture everyone they could find for extermination. I remember the moment we heard them running in looking for us. We virtually stopped breathing, and everybody's eyes converged on one face, that of a little baby in its mother's arms. The slightest sound coming from this infant would have meant the end for us all. I clearly remember holding my breath and praying not to be found and taken by the drunken SS gang.

A thought flashed through my mind – if there were Jewish children at that very moment living in freedom far away in Palestine, why was I not one of them? Could it be true that there were children, Jewish children, somewhere in the world quite free to be what they were, with no one chasing them and their parents, no one hurting them and horrifying them? I remember that feeling of disbelief and, at the same time, longing for such a liberation. It seems that to this day, so many years later, somewhere very deep inside me is lodged a distrust in any possibility of a free, peaceful existence – the distrust forced on me during that time which should have been the flowering of my childhood.

In some inexplicable way throughout all these situations which I remember now, a thin independent thread wove itself: that of my musical talent coming up now and again for expression. Somehow from time to time I played a little, although not, of course, during the ghetto days, especially as most of our belongings had been taken away before we were forced out of our original home. I had no piano and there were still more experiences awaiting us before I happened to come near a piano again.

CHAPTER 3

In the Ghetto and Escape

My sister Frydzia, who was barely 16 at the time, was forced, together with other adults, to do factory work for the Germans. Wearing the blue Star of David on a white band around her arm (to distinguish her from the so-called 'normal' Aryan world), she had to report by the ghetto gate very early each morning to be taken to work on a lorry guarded by uniformed Germans. In the evening the lorries arrived back at the ghetto and unloaded all the workers to spend the night within its walls. My sister was a very sensitive, artistic, intellectually alert girl who, prior to these events, went to a very select school. All that, of course stopped and she was forced to do physical work under a regime of terror, with little food and, worst of all, no assurance that her life would be spared.

One day after being loaded on to the lorry that usually drove her back to the ghetto, she, together with her companions, was driven instead to the central railway station in Lwów. There, all the people were told to leave the lorries and get on to a platform where they had to wait in rows of four. All of them were, of course, wearing the white arm band with the blue Star of David. Guarding them closely were armed SS men. Gradually more and more lorry-loads of Jewish people were brought to the station to join those already standing in rows. All these people were to be put into the windowless cattle trains to be transported to an unknown destination. Nobody spoke, but most of them realised that their last hour was near.

I can only guess what my sister went through in her state of helplessness. Or perhaps I am being presumptuous in thinking that I can imagine her real feelings at that time. All I know is that the circumstances of that event led to the awakening in her of an irrepressible drive towards finding a way out of our doomed situation in the ghetto.

Frydzia was standing in one of the rows of people, when another lorry arrived at the station. Suddenly an older woman from among the new arrivals called out 'Frydzia, what are you doing here? Get out! You must get out!' My sister suddenly acted as if put under a spell by this woman, who turned out to be the mother of a boyfriend from school who had been deeply in love with Frydzia; he had died not long before from meningitis. The woman, widowed and bereaved of her only child, seeing my sister amongst the row of 'lambs for slaughter', must have exerted an extraordinarily powerful influence over her to persuade her to attempt an escape from a situation from which no one could have dreamt of coming out alive. The hypnotic power of the woman's voice gave this frightened and helpless young girl sudden courage to attempt the impossible. She began to move out of her row of four to the one behind, then to the next, watching carefully the Germans who guarded them with machine guns. She managed to retreat from each successive row when the guard looked in another direction. She finally arrived in the last row (others moving into her place) and at the moment the guard looked away she swiftly pulled off the Star of David arm band, picked out a bunch of violets which a peasant woman was selling from a basket nearby, and walked right out of the station as if she had nothing to do with all the gathered Jews. Once out, she ran as fast as she could, and ran a vast distance, ending up outside the city. She wandered in the fields throughout the night, hid in the dark in a remote barn, and before dawn managed to find an opening in the ghetto wall through which she stole her way back to us.

Meanwhile, my parents had heard that Frydzia had been taken with a transport of people who were brought to a place in the country – some hundreds of them – stood in a row, and made to dig a ditch into which they were shot. They were all then buried in the ditch, with some people not yet dead. That was the unimaginable fate my brave sister miraculously managed to escape. Mother was quite certain she would never see her again and was totally distraught. And I, though quite little at the time, felt the measure of her despair and my own great sense of loss at the realisation that I should never see my only sister again. Then suddenly, at dawn, as if returning from the other world, exhausted, dirty, almost wild with anxiety and anger, she appeared. All of a sudden, the innocent girl had changed into a determined fighter. 'We must escape! They will not get us for slaughter! We must get out of this prison!' she kept calling out to my parents.

There was only one thought dominating her existence at that time: the search for a way of escaping from the ghetto. She must have generated such intensity of feeling that it somehow pushed my parents, or perhaps especially my mother, towards taking definite steps to make contact with people who were outside the ghetto – Jews and Christians involved in helping to save the lives of Jewish people. I was not aware of the way in which these contacts were made, but they did lead to our eventual escape from the ghetto.

One of my mother's brothers, Max the youngest, who managed to hide amongst some Christian people and not be sent to the ghetto, lived with his wife and young son under a fictitious non-Jewish name. He was probably the wealthiest member of our family and a man of great awareness of the situation and the needs of his relations and of other people. This remarkable man used much of his money to try and save as many lives as he could, by buying false identity papers for them to be able to live as non-Jews. This he also did for us.

Through the bravery, intelligence and imagination of a friend of the family, a psychiatrist by the name of Leopold ('Poldi') Richter, the attempt to get us out of the ghetto and save our lives was undertaken. Dr Poldi (as he was called by all of us) was from Czechoslovakia and educated in the German language. For that reason, while living in Poland he was able to hide his Jewish identity and pass himself off as a German national. He was a very gifted and clever man with close links with my Uncle Max. Poldi supplied resourcefulness, imagination and courage, while Max was able to offer the badly needed financial support.

Dr Poldi's qualities are well illustrated by an incident he later recounted to us. This concerned a train journey he was making from Switzerland to Germany around 1943. At the border an SS controller came into his compartment to check his documents and, seeing a suitcase on the rack, asked what was in it. Poldi cheekily replied 'Oh! a whole lot of false passports!' The German official surprisingly saw the humour of it, didn't pursue his question any further and left the compartment. The suitcase did indeed contain a number of false passports which Poldi was going to use to help Jews hide their identity. In fact, during the occupation, Poldi had saved a number of Jewish people from extermination. He had done so by disguising himself as an SS officer – as when he brought my mother and me out of the ghetto – as well as arranging false passports.

Poldi worked in a hospital in Lwów and one of the nurses, a Catholic woman who was obviously very much in love with him, stood by him and helped in every way she could. It was with these two people that my sister made contact after her miraculous escape from the extermination 'transport'. They set to work in arranging false identity papers for each one of us – these were in fact genuine identity cards (every citizen of Nazi-occupied Poland had to carry one). They gave information such as date and place of birth, religion – the most important paragraph – and various other details of identity, which in our case were, of course, untrue.

To have a paper proving that we were Christians was of vital importance. But the most essential step was to break out of the ghetto walls and find ourselves in comparative freedom on the 'Aryan' side of the town. I say comparative because all the townspeople, not only the Jews, were under the Nazi jackboot. Escape meant coming out of 'the cell of the condemned'.

Dr Poldi, together with the nurse in whose apartment he stayed, first helped my sister to escape the ghetto, and took her in. Then, with the help of Uncle Max's money, he made arrangements to get papers corresponding to my mother's and my ages and we were brought out under his protection. Poldi's way of rescuing us from the ghetto was to dress in the uniform of an SS officer – we never knew how he came by it – and, as he was bringing Mother and me past the heavily armed guards, to fool them by telling them, in his strong high-class German, that he was getting rid of us and that anyway there was typhus in the ghetto. Poldi must have been so convincing that the guards did not see the illogicality of his not just leaving us to die of typhus in the ghetto. These were our first steps out of the imprisonment of the condemned, and the prospect of certain death.

He had plans to get my father out only two days later but, alas, it was not to be. My father, in the prime of his life, still only in his thirties, was taken away to the city prison where many atrocities took place. There, eventually, he was executed. I knew nothing of that at the time. My mother kept it from me and never mentioned anything about my father's whereabouts or his fate. I was to learn of it only many years later – I was then just over 40 – when I first gathered the courage to ask my sister directly what had happened to Father. She looked surprised that I did not know and told me he had been executed at the notorious Janowski prison in Lwów.

At the time of our escape from the ghetto we were continually watchful, on guard against the ever-present danger of being identified as Jews trying to escape the fate pre-destined for us by the Nazis. We existed in the shadow of death, in fear of being caught. In such conditions, I can see how my mother was too frightened to add another dimension to my already enormous load of anxiety by telling me of the loss of my father.

Many years after the war I discovered that my sister who, at the time of Father's execution was in hiding at the house where Dr Poldi and the Polish nurse lived, had an almost suicidal reaction on hearing what had happened. She broke down and yelled uncontrollably, so that Poldi and his friend were very concerned about her safety in case neighbours discovered who she was and why she had got into such a state. I am now quite convinced that the many severe states of emotional illness which she experienced years after the ending of the war had their roots in those events, and that one of the greatest injuries she suffered was that of losing Father and of losing him in such circumstances.

CHAPTER 4

Continual Hiding

The escape from the ghetto of the three of us (Mother, Frydzia and me) was a crucial moment in our quest for survival in those dark years. However, it was only the beginning of a chain of events, each one of them carrying with it the danger of extermination. Dr Poldi accomplished what he set out to achieve in getting us out of the ghetto imprisonment and into the Aryan world of comparative freedom, away from the danger of imminent death. He took us to his apartment for some days. There we underwent a 'crash' course of instruction in how to behave like Catholics in that predominantly Catholic country with a very strictly religious (often superstitious and bigoted) population. One false step in our behaviour amongst strangers could have thrown suspicion on us as escaped Jews, leading to our being denounced to the Gestapo. And no one ever left their hands alive.

We learned the daily routine of basic prayers. We were taught how and when to cross ourselves, how to enter a church and how to participate in a Catholic mass. All that had

been totally unknown to us; the Jewish and Catholic traditions in Poland were quite separate and alien to each other.
Only years after the war did I realise what a step it was for my
mother to abandon her Jewish religious ways (although only
outwardly) in order to save the lives of her children first of
all, as well as her own – the latter perhaps mainly for our sake.

After some days in hiding, preparing for acting out our
new identity, it was decided that Mother should take me with
her and travel to the capital, Warsaw. My sister, under her new
name Janina Gruszczynska, would stay behind in Lwów for
the time-being. In Warsaw, we hoped it would be easier to pass
unnoticed by anyone who might have known us previously
and could have denounced us as Jews to the Gestapo. Uncle
Max, then living under the false name of Stanislaw Gabrysiak,
provided the money for Mother's new fictitious papers. He
also gave sums of money to help us set up home elsewhere
in the country. Mother's new name, according to her false
papers, was Aniela Zachaczewska. All details relating to her
place of birth, her parents and, most importantly, her religion,
were quite fictitious. I, also under the name of Aniela, was
included in her 'kenkarte' (identity card) which was the most
important legal document of every citizen of Poland during
the Nazi occupation, and had to be available to be checked at
any time or place.

It is an extraordinary fact that we were marked out for
total extermination although, apart from following a different religion, we were not really different from other Polish
people. Indeed, by taking on false names and false data
about our religion we were assumed to be normal humans
worthy of staying amongst the living. Equipped with these

papers, our newly acquired Catholic education and almost no belongings, except the clothes we were wearing and just one or two other small personal items, Mother took me to the main railway station of Lwów. From there we were to take a train to Warsaw where Uncle Max was in hiding together with his wife and son, Mitek with his wife's mother and sister. He was to give us both money and advice on what to do and where to go to find a safe roof over our heads.

That particular occasion has stayed in my memory most vividly. Mother and I arrived at the main railway station. She had tickets for a train to Warsaw. The journey was to take all night. We were to leave at around eight o'clock in the evening and arrive in Warsaw early the following morning. We came on to the platform and stood in front of a train for some minutes waiting, I know not for what. At the moment the train on our platform began slowly to move away, my mother turned to one of the railway attendants and asked when the train for Warsaw was leaving. The man looked at her with some amazement and said, 'My dear woman, the train which just left this platform was the one you are asking about. There is no other train going to Warsaw tonight.' My mother looked extremely upset on hearing this, which prompted the man to try to help her in some way. He then mentioned that if she could speak German the stationmaster, who was of course German, might put us on the midnight train to Warsaw running specially for German officers.

Mother's heart sank. She felt caught between two threatening possibilities. Firstly, to admit that she spoke German fluently – which she did, having gone to school in Graz in Austria – could throw suspicion on us. It was commonly known that hardly any Poles spoke German, although many Jews did, partly because Yiddish is based on medieval German. (The foreign language spoken by educated people in Poland of the pre-war and wartime periods was mainly French.) Secondly, the prospect of being put onto a train with only German officers was as attractive as being thrown into a lion's den. Yet we had to get to Warsaw and Mother could not admit her fears to the railway man who at that moment was trying to help her, without his realising who she and her little girl really were. Mother made up a lie about knowing 'only a few words' in German, whereupon the man took us to the stationmaster's office.

The German stationmaster must have felt quite isolated amongst Polish workers who spoke no German at all, so that on hearing my mother's few words of his language he immediately became very friendly, invited us to sit in his own office, brought us refreshments and insisted we stay in his room until the arrival of the officers' train for Warsaw. We had over three hours to wait until then and, in our situation, there could not have been a safer place than the seclusion of the stationmaster's office where no SS men would come in to look for fugitive Jews who had escaped from the ghetto. And search they did, several times on that occasion, ruthlessly dragging away people whom they suspected to be Jewish. The fact is that there were, at that time, literally hundreds of desperate Jewish people who had realised that the ghetto would soon be totally destroyed and its inhabitants either killed on the spot or sent to extermination camps.

Many made attempts to break out of the ghetto. Some managed to hide in various ways amongst the Christian population, often with the help of costly fictitious documents such as ours. Others were less lucky and fell into the hands of the SS after only a short while away from the ghetto. Many were indeed caught at public places, particularly railway stations from which they tried to travel away from their home town. My mother and I were in exactly this category except that, by chance, we happened to be well away from the dangerously exposed areas of the station, being entertained more or less as personal guests of a German stationmaster.

At around midnight the stationmaster led us out of his office onto the platform at which a train arrived carrying only passengers in German uniform. He took us personally into a compartment of several Gestapo officers and, after some friendly words, left us in their care! They were very polite, addressed my mother in German and made room for us in the compartment. As it was so late at night they thought that her little girl (who was shivering with immense inner fear) ought to lie down. They all moved to one side of the compartment and made me lie down on all three seats on the other side, providing one of their hateful green uniform overcoats in place of a blanket to cover me warmly. They were men of the Gestapo whose main task at that time was to play an active part in the extermination of the Jews . . . Yet here they were treating a small Jewish girl with kindness and consideration only because they had no idea who she really was . . . Oh, how shameful is the stupidity of the conditioned mind. These same Gestapo officers would have been quite happy to shoot my mother and me on the spot if they had discovered we were Jewish. No further proof of crime was needed. The fact of being born Jewish constituted an indisputable reason for our extermination in the eyes of these men insane with Nazi ideology.

That night's journey displayed the enormous tragedy of this farce of the executioners unknowingly giving full protection and displaying charming friendliness to the two of us who could otherwise so easily have been their victims. Throughout the journey, however, I felt a chilling fear, particularly because of coming into such close proximity with these dreaded figures in their uniforms which had become to me symbols of death.

The night wore on and early next morning we arrived at Warsaw's main station. Needless to say, I had not slept for a moment, being so anxious throughout the night. The Gestapo in our compartment said a friendly farewell to us and my mother took me by the hand and walked through the station towards the street. As we were passing the main station hall we overheard some Polish people telling each other how the Germans had stopped last night's train from Lwów to Warsaw and discovered great numbers of Jews escaped from ghettos who were trying to smuggle their way into Poland's biggest city – its capital, Warsaw. It was that very train which my mother had looked at while waiting on the platform in Lwów. It was that train we, for some strange reason, had missed and were therefore put into the safe hands of our Gestapo 'guardians'. This was one of a whole chain of incidents where death slipped by leaving us untouched.

That strange journey over, we found ourselves in the middle of a new, large city with nowhere to go except a hotel recommended by my Uncle Max. By then he and his family were hiding amongst some non-Jewish people in the city. Our only contact with him could be by telephone with cryptic messages being exchanged so as to avoid any possible recognition. He supplied my mother with money and gave what advice he could, but we never went to see him in case one of us was recognised, so endangering the lives of all the others. This was the pattern of contacts between all of us, who were escaping and hiding. Most of the telephone conversations between my mother and her brother were conducted as if it were in code. She would describe to him what her problems were and talk about herself as a third person. It always sounded like a discussion about someone else.

'Hello, this is Aniela,' she would say, using her assumed name, 'I saw the sister of Stanislaw; she and her daughter came in by train this morning. She does not know where she should go now. I wonder what you think . . . ?'

CHAPTER 5

Arrival in Warsaw

We spent the first night in Warsaw in a hotel, which provided no let up in our fear-ridden state. We heard lots of commotion and shouting of the Germans who, as we learned the next day, were taking Jewish people who were hiding in neighbouring houses. These were the unfortunate individuals whose outward appearance was so obviously Semitic that their real identity could not be hidden. My mother and I spent the night in great fear that we would be recognised and taken away. I could hardly sleep and when I did fall asleep for a while I wet my bed, which caused shock and embarrassment to us both as I had not been at all given to such accidents since early childhood. However, we were spared the dreaded fate of being captured on that occasion and the following day Mother began to look for some permanent accommodation for the two of us. She found something on the outskirts of Warsaw, in a type of workers' residential suburb called Kolo. The area was comprised of streets of little uniform-looking houses with tiny front gardens, occupied by working and lower middle class people. One of the families offered to let a room to us for a fair rent. The room was, in fact, half of their home, which consisted of that one fairly large all-purpose room and a kitchen of about the same size. The entrance to the apartment – one of a bungalow-type terrace of similar apartments – was through a few square yards of small garden running into a porch that led to the kitchen, which was divided in half by a full-length curtain.

The Topolski* family, whose apartment it was, consisted of the mother, a middle-aged woman trained as a primary school teacher, a little girl of my age called Jola, another daughter, Alicja, who was nearly 20, and a son in his early twenties called Zygmunt. The father worked at the post office in the parcel department, though at the time of our arrival he was serving a prison sentence for having stolen some food parcels from the post. He was in fact the only breadwinner for the family as his wife was out of work and the grown-up children did not bring in very much. Mrs Topolska had decided to let their only room for a monthly payment which was supposed to help their financial situation. The idea was a good one, except that it meant that the whole of their family had to find a way of living and sleeping in the kitchen, though admittedly a fairly large one. They were however stretching its possibilities beyond its limits.

Mother and I were received very eagerly by the family as their lodgers. We followed my uncle's advice that we should find a room with a family; he was of course paying for everything, since we had no possessions and no money to live on. Mother kept in touch with him constantly through

---

* Mr Topolski – masculine form
Mrs Topolska – feminine form
The Topolskis – plural or collective form

their 'coded' phone calls and he supplied us with money via some special friends, non-Jewish of course.

Our life at the home of the Topolski family started off with the two of us living in our rented room, while the Topolskis lived in their kitchen which they had subdivided into a sleeping area and an area for cooking. It took only a very little time before my mother suggested to Mrs Topolska that she and her little girl Jola join us and move their beds into 'our' room. Soon our meals were also shared. In fact, eventually, it was my mother who more or less fed the family as they had hardly any income except the rent we paid them. This arrangement would have been farcical in normal times, but for us at the time it seemed a God-sent life-saving situation. The Topolskis put it about that we were related to them. Jola called my mother 'Auntie Aniela' and I called her mother 'Auntie'. Being so closely linked to an obviously Christian family added a sense of security to our otherwise always dangerously precarious situation.

For a little while our life had a degree of peace, though the underlying fear and anxiety about being found out never really left us. There was another source of worry for Mother particularly; the fact that my sister stayed in Dr Poldi's house in Lwów and we had only occasional letters from her. Father was never mentioned to me anymore.

At the Topolskis I became friendly with my contemporary, Jola. We played games together, and went to church together. I had by then become totally familiar with Catholic customs and prayers, both at home and in church. With Jola I used to join a group of children playing various outdoor games, for there was much outdoor activity amongst the children in this neighbourhood of small family homes and apartments.

People had tiny gardens in front of their kitchens where they grew vegetables or kept chickens or rabbits. The staple diet consisted of dishes based on potatoes, beetroot, cabbage and onion. There were very small rations of some meats, very few eggs, a little sugar (mostly we used saccharine) and a few other very basic food products. Anything of slightly better quality was either completely unavailable or could only be obtained for a very high price on the black market. (In this respect the situation continued in Poland for long years after the Nazi occupation ended.)

However, these deprivations in one's daily existence were nothing to us Jews whose problems were not just what to eat but how to survive from day to day, or often hour to hour. In our own case the generosity of Uncle Max (or Staszek, as we came to call him according to his fictitious new Christian name) enabled us to have sufficient money for the food we could get. In fact, Mother began to cook more, so that the other people in the family ate with us – particularly little Jola and her mother.

At that time my mother insisted on my memorising some vital bits of information, such as Uncle Max's telephone number and, for some strange reason, the full name and address of her sister in New York. She also insisted that if anyone should denounce us to the Nazi authorities I should pretend that I was not her child, so that if they took her away I could contact my uncle and help to save her. I think that even at that young age I saw through these plans that Mother made and realised how she was trying to safeguard against the possibility of my being killed. There was no doubt in anyone's mind that if a Jewish person was discovered hiding, or passing themselves off as a Christian under a false name, there was only one outcome for him or her – death.

My tender age did not prevent me from maturing abnormally quickly in some respects. I listened to everything said around me and understood well the dangers we were exposed to at every step. I learned to be on my guard whenever questions were asked relating to my family, my past home or my father. Mother's story was that Father had been killed on the front when Hitler first invaded Poland. We were supposedly of a very simple background so we always tried to talk as little about ourselves and our past as possible, as it was all a complete fiction. There was always the risk of being caught out on something we did not know how to lie about.

During our time at the Topolskis, very friendly and cordial relations developed between us. They were charming, well-educated people who at that time suffered from considerable poverty. There was another serious problem afflicting almost their entire family and that was vodka. Mrs Topolska was drinking increasingly more, secretly drawing on her meagre housekeeping money, though we all could tell that she was doing this. She even began to sell whatever she could in order to obtain money for vodka; sadly, she even sold a pair of her little daughter's shoes. Her drink problem became an uncontrollable compulsion. Yet she remained always warm and friendly with only occasional outbursts of despairing moods. The drinking literally helped to 'drown her sorrows'.

Drinking vodka to excess has always been a widespread national problem in Poland. Naturally in times of such stress as life under Nazi occupation, drinking flourished.

Vodka was expensive and not always obtainable; therefore substitutes were found. One of these was a very potent home-brew extracted from potato peelings, which were always in sufficient supply. This drink was called '*biber*' (pronounced 'beeber'). Our friends, Mrs Topolska and her son Zygmunt, also took to drinking *biber*. It was sad to see all of this happening around us; the misery brought about by alcohol and alcoholism intensified by the general misery of daily life.

In the midst of that family situation my mother and I lived in a constantly watchful state, guarding carefully the truth of our real identity, watching whether someone was becoming suspicious of who we were and how and why we were living with the Topolskis. Mother did not go out to work, which in a neighbourhood of working people with living on very limited means, made her an obvious object of suspicion.

The Topolski family never let us think that they guessed we were not who we were pretending to be. It had by that time become common knowledge that many thousands of Poland's three million Jews had made attempts to break out of the ghettos in various parts of the country. Many were attempting to acquire fake documents – usually for enormous sums of money to prove their 'Christian' or in any case 'Aryan' identity. Very many of them found their way to Warsaw where they, like us, were hoping to pass unrecognised in the crowd. Our Topolski family knew that only too well and soon after meeting us they must have put two and two together and realised who we really were. It was lucky for us that they proved to be courageous and humane enough not only to not hand us over to the Gestapo, but also to help us by pretending to outsiders that we were related, all the while never letting on to us that they guessed anything about our true identity. I said that they were courageous, because the Nazis treated people who knowingly (or even unknowingly) hid Jews as traitors, and punished them accordingly – usually by execution.

One small incident during the early period of our stay with the Topolskis indicated to Mother and me that they realised we were probably Jewish escapees from the ghetto. What is more, they had guessed from which ghetto we must have escaped. On one occasion, when the weather was cold and the windows of the kitchen were covered in a thick layer of steam, Zygmunt Topolski, who was my senior by at least 12 years, light-heartedly teased me. He pointed to the window and slowly wrote in the steam the word 'Lemberg'. My heart sank. Young as I was I knew immediately that he was testing me to confirm his suspicions about our origin and identity. Lemberg is, of course, the German name for Lwów, from where we had indeed escaped.

How did he guess this? Quite simply from traces of our regional accent in Polish. There were ways of pronouncing certain syllables which were unmistakably characteristic of people living in Lwów. Zygmunt, a very bright, intelligent young man, found no difficulty in spotting this in our way of speaking. Added to the fact that Mother seemed to have sufficient money for our modest needs without going out to work, our accent completed for him the puzzle about us. I was frightened but did my best to pretend that I had not noticed his subtle hint and went on with some game we were playing at the time as if I was completely engrossed in it.

While living in Kolo with the Topolskis I became very attached to my new friend Jola. We played together, made up games, and produced shows for the family using the kitchen's dividing curtain as an imaginary stage curtain, and with chairs, tables, and brooms for scenery. There were moments of great fun. We played with other children from the neighbourhood, went to church and even, when the time came, took our first communion together. I now know that my mother found this very painful because it felt to her like a sinful betrayal of her faith and heritage, but she went along with it to help to save our lives – mine especially.

We had to go along with all the customs followed by the people around us. Many of the Catholic traditions observed at home included saying the 'paternoster' every evening whilst kneeling by the bed and looking at a picture of the Virgin Mary, Christ, or a patron saint. We of course had to go to mass every Sunday. My mother somehow managed to avoid the painful charade of taking communion, which was something too dishonest for her to go through. However, a time came when I absolutely had to do what all little girls in the neighbourhood did, including Jola. This was arranged for a number of girls of our age on the same Sunday. We were all dressed in white; somehow a suitable white fabric was found for Jola and me. We wore flower chains in our hair and veils, and generally looked like little brides. Of course confession had to precede communion, so the day before I had made up a list of suitable 'sins' to confess to the priest.

At confession, the priest would listen behind his screen and then assign a suitable penance for the sins. Often that would take the form of saying a certain prayer a number of times, or repeating the rosary several times. All these ceremonies were deeply impressive and I am certain that were it not for my having constantly to be on guard against being recognised as a little Jewess, I would have gradually been won over to following the Catholic faith. In fact, some part of it did genuinely touch me.

A time came, after a few months, when the father of the Topolskis was released from prison. He came home and proved to be another warm and friendly member of the family. He was also partial to drinking quite generous amounts and, although he obviously came to like us quite genuinely, his drinking had its potential dangers for us. Some people, keen on getting rid of every possible Jew in sight and collecting a financial reward for denouncing Jews, began to watch us with suspicion. Of course, Mother and I did not know about this at the time.

My constant insecurity and fear of being put to death should our true identity be discovered was intensifying, with no real prospect of any respite. One day, at a point of experiencing particular panic, I spontaneously sought succour from prayer. Knowing that my mother trusted her own traditional Jewish faith and was very keen on my remaining faithful to that tradition too, she would be upset to see me turning to the church. I therefore went in secret and chose the chapel of St Theresa to pray for her protection of us. Something made me choose that particular saint from amongst the various others whose chapels were in the local church. I was just over nine at the time.

———❀———

Many years later, while travelling through central Spain with my husband Roger, as we celebrated our 25th wedding anniversary, my memory of my 'petition' to St Theresa was reawakened. At one point, we unexpectedly found ourselves in Avila, the place at the centre of St Theresa's spiritual activities. I was deeply moved and, in tears, told Roger about my childhood prayers to her. When we returned to England Dr. Andrew Goldstein, the remarkable Rabbi of the Liberal Synagogue to which I belong, gave me a book on the life of St Theresa. From it I discovered that St Theresa was the granddaughter of a Jew who had been forced to convert to Christianity during the Spanish Inquisition in the fifteenth century. How poignant. No such offer was even considered by the Nazis, whose only aim was the total annihilation of all Jews.

———❀———

One day while I was out playing with a group of children in the street, a little girl pulled me aside and to my horror asked me in a lowered voice whether I was Jewish. 'Do tell me; I will not tell anyone about it', she said. My knees almost gave way. I began to shake inside and felt like a trapped animal. Within a few seconds a self-protecting reaction came up in me. I pretended not to have heard her question and ran back to the group of children from which she had drawn me aside. I began to jump and talk loudly about something, trying to get the attention of the other children and making sure that she could not get another chance to speak to me alone. That evening when Mother gave me supper I could not eat. I was in a state of great inner panic and in my innocence thought that I had to protect Mother from anxiety and therefore did not tell her what had happened. Mother began to notice that something was wrong; my appetite had gone, I was behaving strangely and appeared to be very tense. When she asked me anxiously if I felt ill or if something was wrong, I pretended all was well. In my own 'logic' and out of concern for my mother I wanted to hide from her the fact that I knew there were people in the neighbourhood who, in a sly way through their own young child, had tried to find out whether we were Jewish. In other words, we were under suspicion and that spelled grave danger. I was very frightened but did not want to upset Mother. Finally, after a few days of hiding the truth from her, I broke down, began to cry and told her what had happened. Mother was quite alarmed but kept a brave face. She reminded me again that if anyone did denounce us to the Gestapo and they tried to take us away, I must at all costs pretend that I was not her daughter and try to stay behind in order to contact Uncle Max and tell him what had happened, so that he could help to get her out. Her scheme for attempting to save me even if she was taken for extermination was quite obvious, but I promised to follow her instructions if possible.

We did not have to wait too long before such a dreaded opportunity presented itself. One day, quite without warning, two men of the Polish militia unexpectedly arrived at the Topolskis' home. The militia were exclusively Polish and subservient to the German authorities, but with less actual power than the Germans. Only my mother and I were in at that moment. They asked us to come along with them after saying that someone had suggested to them that we were Jews in hiding. Mother at first put on an amazing show of incredulity at what she called 'people's stupidity' in thinking and talking such nonsense. However, when she realised that the militia men were obviously unconvinced by what she had to say and would take us both to be interrogated, she made a courageous attempt at buying them off with a substantial sum of money which, luckily, Uncle Max had just sent to her. It was risky to try and do that, but to our enormous relief the men took it. They then said: 'We are willing to believe you (!), but it might be better for you not to stay here because people talk. . .'

That incident was our second narrow escape from falling into the hands of those who wished to destroy us. It left us in a state of shock, not knowing where to go next. We had thought that perhaps our quiet corner in the Topolski household would see us through to some eventual ending of the period of horror. We wondered what had led to the visit of the militiamen. Mother was convinced that it must have been caused by some drunken remark of Mr Topolski, who used to meet with his friends for drinking sessions. She suspected that at some point while drunk he must have said that with his family lived a 'lovely Jewess with her child'. He was extremely kind and friendly to us and would never have meant to harm us, but letting his tongue loose among his drinking companions would have started the gossip spreading until it was picked up by some stooge of the Nazis who sent the militia to us. That incident unfortunately had to bring to an end our stay with the Topolski family.

CHAPTER 6

A Brief Haven of Peace

Once more Mother turned for advice to Uncle Max, who suggested that it might be best and safest for her to find a family who wanted a housekeeper-cum-maid. There were still some wealthy Polish families living in the capital who employed servants and kept them separate from the family, so they were quite inconspicuous. It was for that reason that the idea seemed right for us, because we wanted to be as little noticed as possible by anyone. The only thing for us to do was to look through newspaper advertisements and search for a suitable position.

Mother took me by the hand and the two of us began going from one place to another asking if they wished to interview her for the housekeeper position they had advertised. But in each case no sooner was the door opened than it shut in our faces; no one wanted to engage a woman with a child. Household after household, day after day, people would open the door, ask what Mother wanted and then looking at me standing by her side would say: 'Sorry, we can't have you with a child'. . . . And so, we would return to the Topolskis' house at the end of each day, tired and disappointed after several such experiences.

Then one day we went to a place situated a little outside Warsaw. It was a beautiful wooded area where some of the wealthy people had villas, surrounded by large gardens and many splendid trees. A single man of about 40 who ran a business in Warsaw had advertised for a housekeeper to look after his attractive home there. Mother took me with her for an interview. The man seemed very sympathetic, did not mind a woman with a child and was glad to have someone who was not just a young, perhaps irresponsible, girl to look after his home while he was away at his business in Warsaw all day. We were greatly relieved. At last there was someone who did want to engage us. The prospect of being able to live in that lovely, secluded house where hardly anybody was ever seen, seemed like a rest and an ideal hiding place for us. There we could hope to be away from people's watchful eyes and maybe find the longed for safe home.

The man received us in a very friendly way, showed Mother round the house, and explained that there was a gardener who looked after the surrounding grounds. There was just one remark he made which Mother thought was strange. He asked her not to chat about the household or about him to any neighbour who might chance to come by. However, at the time Mother did not make much of what might have been behind his slight apprehension. She was more than willing not to speak to anybody for fear of falling under suspicion herself.

We moved in. The place became for us a haven of peace and beauty of nature. We were alone all day in the house

and had lovely living quarters; what a change of surroundings from the frugal home of our friends the Topolskis!
(Incidentally, they remained in close contact with us at this
time and were very sad at our leaving them.)

My mother looked after the house and prepared dinner for
our employer who would come home in the evenings, almost
always bringing some small gift for me. It was peaceful; life
ran quietly from hour to hour. We met no one except the
gardener, who did not pay much attention to us. We could
not believe that life could be like that after the horrors and
anxiety we had experienced previously. The entire situation
seemed like some unreality, a dream. This lasted for about
two weeks. Then one day a young woman came to speak to
our employer (whose name eludes me). He received her in his
study and had a conversation with her, after which he asked
my mother to let her have some things the young woman
had in his house. He then spoke to her for a while before she
finally left. This was at the beginning of a weekend.

The following day the man's behaviour seemed totally
changed; a cloud of tension seemed to have descended upon
him and he appeared aloof and not very communicative.
Finally, at the end of the day he called my mother into his
study. He looked at her and said: 'Mrs Zachaczewska, I know
that you are Jewish, please don't try and deny it. Your real
name is Podhoretz and you come from Lwów, where your
older daughter went to the Hebrew High School. I know
many details about your real identity but you need not fear. I
shall not denounce you to the Gestapo.'

My mother was so shocked at hearing all this that she
dissolved into floods of tears, feeling quite helpless and

vulnerable. Of course, there was no point in denying anything he had said, since he obviously knew a lot about us. It
was so utterly unexpected and astounding. How did he find
out? He reminded Mother of the young woman who came to
collect some things from his house the previous day. Mother
had met her briefly while looking with her for her belongings,
which she had left in the store room. Afterwards, the young
woman went back to our employer's study and at that point
decided our fate. She had been employed by this man before
us; he recognised that she was a fugitive from a ghetto and
asked her to leave. Now, on returning to collect her things she
discovered that her ex-employer had unknowingly engaged
as his new housekeeper not only a Jewish woman, but one
with a child, a woman whose elder daughter she knew well
from school in Lwów.

So, that was how the whole story of who we really were
came to his knowledge. The young woman had told him
everything she knew about us, including our real name.
There was no sense in denying the facts my mother was told
by him. She just sat and cried. He seemed very sympathetic
and assured her that we had nothing to fear from him; on the
contrary, he would help us in any way he could, certainly
financially if we needed it. Just one thing was impossible and
that was our continuing to live in his home. He seemed very
firm about that and anxious that we should leave, more or
less straightaway. We were shaken and once more faced the
vulnerability and complete insecurity of our situation.

The two weeks we spent in that lovely home, in peaceful
and beautiful surroundings were a haven in the midst of so
much horror. The only visitor had been a young woman,

whom he called his girlfriend. It all came to an abrupt and totally unexpected end. We had to leave quickly – our employer was very insistent on that. My mother later became convinced that he himself was hiding under a false identity and that his so-called 'girlfriend' was actually his daughter and that obviously, it was far too dangerous for him to keep other ghetto fugitives in his house.

We had to go back to the Topolskis and back to answering newspaper advertisements for housekeepers and maids. However, a position turned up almost immediately. A young couple living in the centre of Warsaw, who shared an apartment with the husband's parents, wanted someone to be their housekeeper-cum-maid-cum-nanny to their two-year-old boy, Jacek. They were willing to engage my mother in spite of her having her nine-year-old daughter with her. The young couple occupied one room, the parents another; both rooms were accessed through the kitchen, the use of which they shared. There was one snag – the two couples had quarrelled and were not on speaking terms at the time we arrived on the scene. We were installed in the kitchen with an iron-framed bed against one wall as our sleeping quarters. A large old-fashioned stove and oven was kept alight in one corner and there my mother cooked together with the mother-in-law of the young Kowalski family. The son went out to some office work; the wife, who had trained as a pharmacist but was unable to work in her own profession, kept a sweet shop in the same building where their apartment was. The young Mrs Kowalska was expecting her second child and was relieved to have my mother to look after her difficult household and her little boy, whom she had to leave at home while she spent whole days at the sweet shop. We were in fact three families (though small ones) squeezed into two rooms and a kitchen.

My mother had a very hard task in coping with the cleaning and cooking, as well as dressing, washing, feeding and generally bringing up the little boy, who was not very easy at times. We lived mainly in the kitchen which overlooked the inner yard of the tall apartment house and its opposite wall with windows from other apartments. This was in the heart of Warsaw on the corner of the street called Krakowskie Przedmieście, which was just some steps away from the Hotel Europejski and the famous café, especially popular with Warsaw's intellectual and artistic circles. I was with my mother all the time and slept with her in one bed.

There were many moments of fear when we knew that the Nazis would suddenly raid a street, fill up a lorry with people who happened to be passing by and drive them to another central street which they would close off. The victims would then be lined up against a wall and shot by a squad of SS men. The day after each such atrocity posters listing the names of the executed would be displayed all over the city. The victims were completely innocent. On the sites of these massacres wreaths would appear and candles were lit. People were absolutely stunned. These were acts of warning to the Polish population or sometimes retribution for underground activity. And there was a growing movement of rebel underground organisations, the biggest of which was the A.K. (Armia Krajowa – National Army). It had many members and, of course, massive support of the population. All this was happening in what we Jews considered to be the 'free' part of Poland. At the same time one ghetto after another was being liquidated with all its inhabitants murdered then and there, or later in extermination camps like Auschwitz, Treblinka, Majdanek and others.

I can clearly remember the constant state of fear and anxiety I experienced day and night. I was of school age and people asked my mother why she did not send me to the local school. She made some excuse about wanting me to help her in the house (schooling was not compulsory). The truth was that the most important thing in her mind was to keep me out of public view in case someone should suspect that I was Jewish. Our dear friends the Topolskis arranged for Jola to visit us several times a week and let me go over with her all the subjects she was studying at school. Mother also insisted that I should read and write each day. I had to sit and copy several pages of writing from books which she chose for me. This was my main form of education at that time.

One day I went with Mother to the coal merchant in our street; Mother had to carry buckets of coal up to the apartment on the second floor where we lived. I stood watching the man filling the two large buckets with coal. He watched me and suddenly said to my mother 'Your little girl is so lovely, she looks just like a little Zydoweczka' (diminutive for 'Jewess'). I shivered inside with panic, but had the presence of mind not to show my reaction outwardly. Later at home we wondered whether he was testing our reactions because he did suspect we were Jewish. By that time our old friends the Topolskis knew the whole truth about us, so we asked them, what could have made people think that I was Jewish? They suggested that although my features were not Semitic, my eyes had an expression which betrayed a specific Semitic quality. I still cannot understand it, but in any case I began to half close my eyelids whenever anyone looked at me. I became very short-sighted soon after the war.

Some while after Mother and I left the Topolski family my sister arrived in Warsaw and went to live with them. She was still in her teens and had to leave Lwów where she had stayed for over a year with Dr Poldi and his nurse friend, who hid her in their apartment after Mother had gone with me to Warsaw. Frydzia (or Janeczka – Jasia for short – as she was then called according to her false identity papers), stayed in Lwów longer than we expected. It later transpired that she and Dr Poldi had fallen deeply in love. My sister's love for Dr Poldi was the first real love of her life. I think that it remained for her one of the deepest feelings she had ever experienced. However, she had to leave Lwów because it was thought that, as with us, it would be safer for her to try and hide in Warsaw. From then on, her contact with Poldi was continued only through correspondence.

His letters would arrive to my mother, who handed them over to Jasia. We used to arrange to meet her in places where no one could see the three of us together. The reason for that was that we looked exceptionally alike (see plates 3 and 9), but unfortunately our false papers were in different names and we had to pretend that there was no family connection between us. In days of such danger, when so many Jewish people were trying to hide in similar ways, we could never risk the chance of anyone suspecting that we were actually both my mother's daughters when, according to our identity cards, only I was. This forced us to meet in circumstances of utmost secrecy and not too frequently. While my sister lived with the Topolski family she told them the truth about who we really were. Her youth and volatile temperament did not let her keep the secret for too long in the company of these friendly people. They responded kindly and courageously, trying to help us in every way they could. Hence their help in my home 'schooling' and the frequent visits they paid to my mother and me at the home of our employers. We continued to call each other auntie, cousin and so on.

My life with Mother at that time centred mainly on the kitchen where she cooked, cleaned, looked after young Jacek and established at first a working relationship, and later a very friendly one with the parents of Mr Kowalski. They must have been in their sixties at the time and although great animosity reigned between them and the young couple, my mother managed to bring them closer and to be on speaking terms again. The young Mrs Kowalska stayed all day in her sweet shop, her husband was out in his office, whereas the older couple spent their days in their part of the apartment. This gave Mother more opportunity to chat with them and befriend them. My mother had a way of endearing herself to people who came into contact with her. In this case, she turned a soured family situation into a much more peaceful one.

Before too long Mother had to look after one more baby; a little girl was born to the young couple. They named her Joasia (short for Joanna). I became Mother's help in looking after her. The poor little infant developed a very severe eczema which covered her face. She seemed to itch constantly and suffered much from it. We had to apply medication to her skin and wrap her tiny hands in layers of delicate fabric which would cause less soreness to her face when she tried to rub her fists against it. We loved the baby and were deeply upset by her condition. Both of us took great care of her and tried to alleviate her obvious great discomfort. She became the main reason for our staying with the Kowalskis.

CHAPTER 7

Trembacka Street, Warsaw

After a while of living in our kitchen at the Kowalski apartment I became increasingly nostalgic for piano playing. This was a passionate involvement and interest that had not been squashed, even by the horror of our situation. I would often see through the kitchen door which led to the old couple's room that there was a piano there. From time to time their daughter who came to visit would sit at the piano and play, admittedly not particularly well.

My desire to get to that instrument and play it made me nag my mother to ask the elder Mrs Kowalska if they would let me play their piano. Mother at first refused to do anything about it. She was indeed very friendly with the old couple but on no account would she let anyone know that I had any musical gifts or had had any previous lessons in music. She wanted to maintain the impression that we came from a simple unsophisticated background. The idea of having a child with a musical gift and ability might have thrown suspicion on us. Musical gifts were so often associated with the Jewish people that my mother lost her sense of proportion in believing that every Christian in Poland would immediately think one was Jewish if one had a musical talent.

She could hardly be blamed for reacting in the way she did, considering the threatening circumstances we were in. However, I was irresistibly drawn to the piano, and insisted that Mother ask old Mrs Kowalska to allow me to play it. Mother at first told me to keep quiet and not ask for such an impossible thing. 'They will begin to suspect us,' she said. 'We must not let on that you have ever played before; we are just simple working-class people, remember'. However, after some time of my constant nagging she approached the senior Mrs Kowalska, who immediately allowed me to come in and play 'at the piano'. I was supposed not to know a thing about it.

The touch and sound of that instrument worked on me like magic. Soon the old couple became intrigued by my playing, which needless to say did not hide the fact that I was musically gifted. They suggested to my mother that when their daughter had her weekly piano lessons at their home from a visiting teacher I should also have lessons. Mother at first refused, saying she did not think 'it was suitable for me to play the piano'. She said I should better spend more time helping with the housework – all that being a flimsy camouflage, hiding her constant fear of being suspected of our Jewish identity. But as was to be expected, she let herself be persuaded and I began to have weekly piano lessons.

The teacher was an old spinster who, we assumed, came from a once wealthy and cultured family who had brought her up in the manner of all well-to-do young women, speaking French and, of course, playing the piano, regardless of whether or not she was musically gifted. Having fallen on hard times during the war, our lady 'teacher' had resorted to giving piano lessons. As a professional pianist and teacher, I can today evaluate her knowledge and teaching ability as almost nil. However, my thirst for music was such that I made enormous leaps from week to week – in spite of rather than because of my teacher. After a while I was playing quite difficult pieces – my repertoire consisted of most of Johann Strauss's waltzes in piano transcription. The piano teacher spoke to my mother and said I was too talented for her to go on teaching me. She suggested that Mother should send me to the famous Chopin school in Warsaw. Naturally my mother received this with a mixture of satisfaction and new anxiety. She absolutely refused to send me out of the house into any public place. The fewer the people who noticed me, or her, the safer we both were.

So once again she found some reason to explain her refusal to send me to the Chopin school. The desperate teacher suggested I should at least play in a little pupils' concert arranged by her friend who taught at the Conservatoire. Mother could not really refuse that, so I did play.

My little performance apparently caused quite a stir. Again, Mother had to show her unwillingness to acknowledge my talent – to avoid any further exposure to people in case my looks or anything about me would cause them to suspect I was Jewish. Sadly, even amongst the more sophisticated Poles, anti-Semitism was so deeply ingrained that anyone was liable to denounce a hiding Jew to the Nazis. My mother's fears of over-exposure were, unfortunately, very justified and well-founded.

My 'lessons' with the old spinster continued. Playing the piano for chosen periods in the day became moments of paradise on earth for me. I indulged in the beauty of the music and the enchantment of the sound of my favourite instrument. This was my contact with an inner world of magic that was quite separate from the terrible reality of the times we lived in.

One of the greatest fears I experienced was that my mother might be killed and I should be left totally alone. This thought was so unbearable that I looked for the means of securing my own death in such an eventuality. I had overheard in some conversation that ink was poisonous. That led me to make a secret plan to drink a bottle of ink if the Nazis ever took my mother away. I did not even consider the possibility of surviving by myself. Yet on occasions it was I who provided encouragement and strength to my mother in moments when she felt it almost impossible to carry on with her struggle for survival.

On one occasion, I heard a commotion amongst the neighbours and looked out at the street from behind the curtains. On the opposite side of our street (which, as I said, was in the very centre of Warsaw) a public execution had just taken place. The street was shut off at both ends and a group of innocent people taken off the streets had been shot against the wall of an apartment building opposite us. All I saw were stains of blood on the building and pavement. The bodies were not there anymore; people had removed them as soon as the Nazis drove away. Some people were lighting candles and putting them on the blood-stained area. My fear of losing Mother was strengthened once more. But for the Grace of

God she might have been one of those unsuspecting innocent people walking along the street who were suddenly taken into an SS lorry and driven to their execution. I felt sick with fear. To this day, it seems to me that I hardly comprehended the full horror of what I saw through the window on that occasion. Yet it was recorded somewhere in my memory and remains as one of the pictures of that period of my childhood.

Our life continued in the household of the Kowalski family with days of comparative quiet and moments of anxiety. One day the young Mrs Kowalska implied that someone had mentioned to her that Mother and I were being suspected of not being who we said we were. She hinted that she was worried about the safety of all of us. (We knew well that a family caught hiding Jews could be executed.) Mother and I lived under a great deal of stress for a few weeks, and then somehow the cloud dispersed.

After hearing from Mrs Kowalska about the danger that she thought we were all in, Mother became exceedingly anxious. It was obvious that we were under suspicion and our lives were once more in a very precarious situation. Mother did not show how very worried and frightened she was – that I only learned later. However, at the time, she told me one morning that she had had an extraordinary dream which made her feel that things would work out favourably for us. In the dream her father came into the kitchen – our little domain at the Kowalskis; he looked at Mother intensely, pacing up and down the length of the place, and then stopped to say: 'Toncia [short for Antonina, her real name], you are worried about the mysterious phone call Mrs Kowalska received. Do not worry; nothing will happen to you; you will be safe!' He repeated the sentence a few times, assuring Mother of our safety and telling her not to worry. Mother woke from the dream with quite an extraordinary sense of confidence, instilled in her by this message from her deceased father. Indeed, days and days went by and we heard no more about the incident. We did not know who the phone call had been from, but it was obvious that we were under suspicion. No harm came to us on that occasion.

However, during those two or three weeks our worries and tension grew to the point that one day Mother, in desperation, put on our coats and took me out into the street. She felt frightened to stay at home in case the Gestapo came for us. This happened only too often to Jewish people in circumstances similar to ours. So many unscrupulous Poles were only too willing to do a bit of 'Jew-detection' for the Nazis and not only get some money for it but probably also the perverse satisfaction of ridding the place of Jews – an added bonus.

At that moment, Mother must have lost heart for the first time since our escape from the Lwów Ghetto. She nervously and aimlessly walked through the streets holding me by the hand. It was almost dark when the curfew started. The Germans, in uniform and armed, began to patrol the streets. No civilian was supposed to be out. Anyone spotted would have been shot without a single question asked. We began a kind of 'cat and mouse' game with the patrolling men from whom we were trying to hide in doorways and dark alleys whenever we saw them. We were not too far from the place we lived at in Trembacka Street. Mother suddenly sat down on a little stone structure, almost collapsed into herself and nearly crying said: 'Oh, I can't go on any more my child. . .

what shall we do?' I remember that moment most distinctly. I embraced her and, trying to calm and reassure her in my innocent child's way, said, 'Mother, don't be frightened, you will see, it will all end all right. I know it will. I know we will not perish, you'll see. Come, let's go back home.' My words must have carried some power in them and my conviction of our unquestionable survival must have communicated itself to Mother and filled her with renewed strength. She got up, embraced me and, carefully avoiding the patrolling Germans, stole her way back to the Kowalskis' home, holding me tightly by the hand. Our life was fraught with such alarms and scares, which fortunately did not end in the way they might have done.

It was during the period we lived with the Kowalskis that the Warsaw ghetto, just a few streets from Trembacka Street, was going through its final stages of gradual destruction amid outbursts of heroic fighting. The Nazis were meeting with desperate and courageous acts of Jewish resistance. There were some links between the ghetto resistance and the Polish underground organisations. It was known that the ghetto inhabitants were not only under constant attacks from the Nazis, but they were suffering complete deprivation. There was almost no food available for them. There were occasions when some individuals from the free side of Warsaw would attempt to throw food parcels over the ghetto walls, while riding past in trams. This was, however, not a frequent event as the hearts of many Poles did not stir easily at the sight of this Jewish tragedy. There came a point when the Nazis were gaining more ground within the ghetto, and what could be seen by the rest of Warsaw was the increasing strength of a red glow over the city's skies which spread from the flames of the burning ghetto. It was an unreal sight, a bloody sight. Warsaw was yet to see much more of this.

We all knew that there was intensive activity going on amongst people connected with resistance organisations, particularly the A.K. (the National Army). Nothing was spoken of openly, but many people, especially the younger ones, were directly or indirectly connected to some underground organisation. There were strong feelings of resentment and hatred towards the Nazis throughout the country. My mother knew that the younger members of the Topolski family, our good friends, were actively involved with the A.K. I only understood it later, as children were kept well away from all the secrets guarded by those who were in any way involved with the resistance. The elder daughter of the Topolskis, Alicja, was engaged to a very charming young man called Felix, who must have brought both her and her brother into the A.K.

By the beginning of 1944, after the complete destruction of the Warsaw ghetto, where not a soul or a home was left, intensive preparations were going on amongst the resistance movements for what was to be the most serious and heroic attempt to hit out at the Nazi occupiers of Warsaw. By that time the Nazis were on the defensive on their main battle front in eastern Europe with the Russian offensive intensifying each day. People's hopes were raised about the prospect of approaching liberation of the country.

Just before the Russians retook the eastern parts of Poland my mother received the last letter from Dr Poldi, written to my sister. Until that moment my mother had always respected my sister's privacy, and passed on her letters unopened, however, on that occasion, for some unknown reason, she felt a compulsion to open and read the letter which she was then to hand to my sister. In the letter was an official, as it were, breaking-off of the commitment and engagement between Dr Poldi and my sister. Without giving any reason for it he asked her not to consider their engagement as valid anymore and therefore assume that they were free of all commitment to each other from then on. My mother was very shaken by this mysterious change of heart on Poldi's part. She knew that he and my sister were deeply in love with each other. She also realised that letting Jasia receive the letter might have given her a shock, which would have led to some emotional reaction, endangering her safety in those precarious times.

Mother made up her mind not to mention to my sister that the letter had arrived. Jasia kept asking about letters, but as the political situation was rapidly changing and the Russians were advancing into eastern Poland, she began to blame the war situation for the lack of correspondence from Poldi. She pined for news from him and never ceased talking about him. Mother kept quiet and resolved never to mention a word about his letter and his apparent change of heart.

Events in Poland began to move with ever greater speed and tension as the German forces began to feel the pressure of offensives on both the Russian and Western fronts. It was known amongst Poland's population that the Russian Red Army was pushing Hitler's forces westwards. Hopes were raised that the Russians might soon liberate us from our ordeal under Nazi occupation. In spite of my young age I picked up a great deal of information about the situation we were all in, from conversations between adults that I over-heard. Everything was spoken about secretively in lowered voices and a hushed atmosphere, yet I gathered what was going on pretty clearly. Occasionally, stories of horrors in Auschwitz, Treblinka, Majdanek and other extermination camps also reached my ears and left undiluted impressions.

The Warsaw ghetto was eventually burnt to the ground.

Once, during the height of its burning, the old Mr Kowalski stood on his balcony, looked at the red inflamed sky over the ghetto and, with an air of satisfaction, turned to my mother saying: 'Well, Hitler at least knew how to get rid of the Jews!' Mother, stunned by this inhuman remark, looked at him and said that Hitler had not yet finished his job and no one could tell whom he would get next. . . (I even think she reproached the old man by calling his remark sinful in the face of so much suffering). She said as much as she felt she could without arousing suspicion over her sympa-thy with the Jews, who after all were being slaughtered so mercilessly without too many tears shed over their fate by some non-Jewish Poles. As it turned out, before too long, my mother's remarks to the old anti-Semite about our not knowing who was going to be next for execution were prophetic for him.

CHAPTER 8

Warsaw Uprising

During 1944, causing serious trouble for Hitler, the Red Army pushed on further and further west. Finally, we could hear the sounds of battle close to Warsaw. The resistance organisations took heart and must have hoped for support from the Red Army, whose offensive brought them eventually to Praga – a part of Warsaw situated beyond the River Wisła (Vistula) which divides the city. In the summer of that year the A.K. and other resistance groups started attacking the occupying Nazi forces.

The Warsaw Uprising had begun. Suddenly we found ourselves in the midst of street fighting in which Polish people of all ages, but particularly the younger (and even very young) ones, began to attack the Germans. They were armed with home-made weapons: obviously no match for Hitler's heavy air and ground forces. Warsaw became a desperate battleground in which the Germans had to fight to recapture each building and every street which they had so 'safely' kept under their occupation. I remember that we were all suddenly engulfed and those of us who were not actively fighting (children like myself, some women and elderly people) spent days and nights in the cellars of the buildings we lived in, trying to escape the shelling, bombing and explosions. My mother, the young Mrs Kowalska with her baby and little boy Jacek, her parents-in-law and I were often huddled in the corner of a large, dark and damp cellar under the apartment house in which we lived. Even there, in the shelter, we could hear the sounds of shooting, of grenades exploding and bombs dropped by the Germans on well-known strongholds of the resistance fighters. We experienced the deprivations of a siege: shortage of food, water, electricity, all basic necessities of daily life. Yet, all that was bearable compared with the constant fear of shelling, explosions and the possibility of being buried alive under the ruins of the building above our heads.

The story of that heroic uprising of the Polish resistance against the Nazi forces in Warsaw has been written about extensively. I can only describe my personal memories of what it was like for a small girl, who was concealing her Jewish identity in a mostly alien society, to be trapped in the middle of this tragic and fierce battle. I was bewildered, even more so than during the quieter period preceding the uprising, when I was constantly on guard against saying something which would disclose my great secret – that secret on which my staying alive depended. The constant inner watchfulness and tension now had the straightforward physical fear of war added to it. It was hard to believe that our situation could have deteriorated to this level of upheaval.

Each hour brought new developments in the fighting. At times members of the resistance fought almost with bare hands, but with desperate determination and hope. The defeat of Hitler was becoming the possibility so deeply longed for. After all, the Red Army had already reached a part of Warsaw. We were expecting them to overpower the Germans who were holding the rest of the city but they obviously had other plans. So, the Russian forces allowed this civilian uprising to take its tragic course. The Germans brought in heavy tanks, planes and large numbers of troops to try to subdue the rebellion. However, it developed to such a pitch that they had to fight for every street and often for every building.

The Nazis became more and more vicious as the days of fighting went on. Not only did they mercilessly bombard the city without regard even for women and children, but they embarked on a road towards the complete annihilation of Warsaw and as many of its citizens as possible. To this end, they took to pouring gallons of petrol over the roofs of the buildings in every street they recaptured from the resistance fighters and setting them alight – sometimes with people still inside. Those who came out of their shelters were pushed out into the streets and, amidst the firing and explosions, made to run to assembly points from where they were taken in railway trucks to an 'unknown' destination – Auschwitz.

My mother's prophetic words were coming true. Now each Polish person who bore a Warsaw stamp on his or her identity card was treated in almost the same way as the Jews had always been. As for Mother and me, the threat of death that had receded somewhat while we were living as 'Aryans' now returned in its full intensity. When German troops stormed into our building, having captured our street, they executed every male they found on the spot. Old Mr Kowalski met the same death he knew about and rejoiced over when it was happening in the ghetto. Depravity, once unleashed, claims any victims in its path. My mother was proved right; old Kowalski was shot on the staircase of our building when the Nazis burst into our apartment houses. The women and children were chased out of the building and made to run, under bullet fire and other explosions, towards the central Theatre Square. There, hundreds of people from different streets of the city centre were arranged into rows, guarded by heavily armed Germans, some of whom were kneeling behind their machine guns, with long belts of shiny bullets by them, ready to fire at the people at any moment. The houses we had been chased out of were set on fire. As we ran, I thought they were going to shoot us down. But as we reached the big square in front of Warsaw's main theatre it flashed through my mind that this was our final execution place. We had run past stacks of human corpses, burned and mutilated; people who must have lost their lives only a little while before we saw their horrendous-looking remains.

I was taking in all these hellish impressions with the acuteness of perception which probably arises only in moments of extreme danger. When we finally came to stand in a line in Theatre Square, facing the machine guns and the fierce and vicious-looking Germans, we were in fact constituting a living barricade through which the fighting continued. I stood in a state of mad panic hanging on to my mother's hand, trying to hide into her body. We were ordered not to move or we would be shot instantly. As it was, bullets were flying through the rows of people, some of whom were hit and dropped wounded or dead. By an extraordinary miracle neither my mother nor I was touched by a bullet. But at one point, facing a machine gun positioned right in front of me, I lost all control and began to cry hysterically, fearing that we should be executed instantly.

It was at that moment that the most extraordinary and unexpected thing occurred. As I stood clutching my mother's dress and shaking with uncontrollable crying, one of the soldiers guarding us came up to me. He ran his hand gently over my head and, in an obviously moved voice, spoke to me in German. Having been exposed to much German spoken amongst my mother's family who had been educated in Austrian schools, I could understand perfectly what he was saying, 'Don't cry dear child, . . . I also have a little girl like you in Vienna. . .' He took from his belt a tin flask containing some coffee. Handing it to me he told me to drink a bit and to give some also to my mother. In this state of absolute distress and fear I automatically hesitated as if I expected his gesture to be some kind of a trap and he was trying to poison us both. I can hardly understand now how these almost demented thoughts flashed so quickly through my mind. The soldier perceived this instantly and took the coffee, drank some of it himself first, then he handed it back to me. His behaviour in those insane circumstances was so astounding that we did not actually comprehend it at the moment. We each drank a few sips. He patted me on the head again with a fatherly tenderness and said, 'Don't be afraid, it will be all right'. The incident seemed absolutely unreal – one of our oppressors and possible executioners coming up to comfort a crying girl. . . We could not really accommodate this experience in the reality of the surrounding madness.

After some hours of standing in rows, surrounded by soldiers, we were more or less pushed into some cellars of the big theatre opposite. There, in crowded cells, we spent the night huddled in groups. From elsewhere in the cellars, the cries of people who must have been tortured reached our ears. We did not know from one moment to the next what our fate was to be. Eventually morning came and an order in German was given for us all to get out into the street – fast. As Mother and I reached the exit my hand was caught by the Austrian soldier, who pushed into it a bag of biscuits and a bottle of coffee saying, 'Take this, you will need it. . .' We did make good use of it later. Then there was a succession of running, waiting, and finally being bundled onto a train. Here a rumour spread: we were going to Auschwitz. I remember most clearly what I felt at that moment – I had heard such descriptions of the atrocities which took place in that concentration camp, that the realisation I was on my way to that hell almost paralysed me with fear. I felt an acute, choking physical pain of fear gripping my entire body. This must have been an experience of the kind of intensity which, in some cases, causes instantaneous death. I cannot describe it any differently.

The train started on its journey out of the fighting city of Warsaw. Ironically, we were being deported, not as Jews, but as citizens of the rebellious capital, as punishment for the uprising against the Nazis. There were almost only women and children and some elderly people on the train. Suddenly. . . it stopped, just a short distance from Auschwitz. The Germans shouted, '*Alle Frauen und Kinder bis fünf jahren, raus!*' ('All women and children up to five years old, out!'). As I was 11 at the time and we were with Mrs Kowalska and her children, she immediately picked up her baby and told my mother to take the boy (the three-year-old my mother had so caringly looked after) so that both Mother and she could legitimately leave the train with a child under five, I sheepishly attaching myself to Mother. We tumbled out of the train, Mother holding little Jacek by the hand and young Mrs Kowalska clutching her baby, Joasia, with me hanging on to Mother's side. We joined hundreds of others and were led to a nearby empty spacious church. The word spread that we were to be locked into the church so that the Germans could set fire to it. There we had to stay overnight, with no food or place to sleep except the concrete floor. We later heard that Auschwitz was too full to take us in. The miracle I had inwardly and desperately begged for on that train journey did happen. We did not get to the gas chambers.

Within a day all the women and children were dispersed out into the countryside and given some food and shelter by people from neighbouring villages. At that point we finally separated from Mrs Kowalska and her two little children. Mother and I found a roof over our heads, offered to us for a few days by some kind people in a village called Pruszków. Within a short time, we were given a cleaned-up and whitewashed room in an outbuilding, which had previously been used as a pigsty. I must mention here that people treated any survivor of the Warsaw Uprising with great sympathy, solidarity and helpfulness. People gave us various supplies of basic clothes, some very elementary bits of furniture, a little primus cooker and a few utensils. All this was accommodated in our little dwelling space in which we were to remain for almost another year.

CHAPTER 9

Pruszków — Semi-Freedom

By some extraordinary coincidence, after being taken out of Warsaw and ending up in a village in its vicinity, we met up again with our devoted friends the Topolski family – or rather, its female members – Mrs Topolska, my little friend Jola, and Alicja, now in her early twenties and unmarried. She was engaged to the very charming young man who was active in the resistance, but had lost contact with him after he joined the fighting in Warsaw. At the time we met Alicja, she was very shaken by her enforced separation from her boyfriend. We also discovered that she was expecting a baby. As soon as we realised that Mrs Topolska and her daughters had no roof over their heads, it was clear that we had to share with them our modest improvised dwelling. The people of the neighbourhood again came to our aid, so that eventually the converted pigsty housed three beds, a little table, and some labourers' stools; we also had our primitive little stove on which we could prepare food. The latter was in short supply in any case and it certainly was of a very limited variety and poor quality. But what did this matter in the face of what we had gone through and were still going through? We accepted such conditions without complaint.

Within days of our release from the train for Auschwitz and our subsequent settling down in Pruszków, we began to be chased again. Once more the Nazis would go into 'action', just as they had in the ghettos. This time, though, they would raid the village streets trying to capture anyone whose identity card showed him or her to be from Warsaw. Such a document became the latest ticket to a concentration camp. We realised that we had been let off the train taking us from Warsaw to Auschwitz only because, on that occasion, there was no more room there to squeeze into it several hundred more humans for extermination. However, within a few days of our release we began to be hunted again. This time the village inhabitants very quickly comprehended our danger and began to do everything they could to prevent us being caught and taken by the SS. We covered the one little window of our pigsty with some grey innocuous-looking cloth, so that no one could guess that there were any humans in that little hut. The village children would run up to give us warning that SS trucks were arriving in search of Warsaw refugees. All five of us would lock ourselves in the hut and, in great fear, wait throughout the raid hoping the SS would not attempt to search it. Mercifully they never did, although this situation lasted from August 1944 until May 1945 when the Nazis were finally defeated and expelled from Poland.

During these months, the fighting in Warsaw gradually subsided. There were great losses among the resistance fighters and the rest of Warsaw's population. The city itself was devastated. The Nazis quite systematically burnt to the ground every building which had not already been destroyed in the street fighting. And all the while the Soviet Red Army stood on the far bank of Warsaw's river and just watched the ongoing destruction. Eventually, by the time the uprising was finally suppressed by the Nazis, Warsaw had become a heap of rubble and ashes. Pockets of resistance continued to struggle for a while, and some people ended up hiding in the sewer system under the city's streets. Many perished there.

After the uprising started Mother and I lost all contact with Uncle Max and my sister Jasia. We had lost hope of ever seeing her again, but while in Pruszków someone put us in touch with a family in another village where my sister was found. This was at the end of 1944. Jasia, who was by now 18 years old, had survived similar ordeals to those experienced by us. She had somehow ended up in this village where she was living with a young couple who were expecting their first baby, and acting as their housemaid. My mother was indescribably grateful to providence to have both her daughters alive and uninjured after all the atrocities we had witnessed and narrowly escaped. Mother often used to say aloud, 'Please God, may I be left absolutely penniless, without any possessions, but with both my children alive'.

Yes, penniless we were indeed and had it not been for the kindness of people around us we would have had nothing to wear for the oncoming winter. We were forced out of our Warsaw home so abruptly and brutally that we ran dressed in whatever we happened to have on at the time; that is, just cotton dresses and light slippers. That was all we had.

No, there was something else, something quite secret and unexpected. I don't really know how I managed to keep it with me, but right through the terrifying time of being taken from our home in Warsaw to the cellars in the theatre, I clutched in my hand a birthday present my father had given me, just before the Nazis came to Lwów. It was a fountain pen and pencil made by Hardtmuth, the firm he represented. The two objects, a brown pen and red automatic pencil, were the last symbols linking me to my father's memory. I clung to them as if they were my only tangible connection to my earlier childhood experiences – of a secure, loving home and, most of all, of my father who had so suddenly vanished from my life and about whom no word had been said to me by anyone, particularly my mother. I never dared to ask about his whereabouts and fate. Possibly somewhere deep inside me I knew the worst, and the circumstances of my own life at the time were so intensely frightening that I kept all inner reality well covered up. Indeed, the question of my father's disappearance remained deeply suppressed in me for many years to come.

However, there was one core part of myself which stayed alive and was not destroyed by all the dreadful events and situations we were engulfed in, and that was my passion for music and piano playing. While still in Warsaw, living with Mother in our corner of the Kowalskis' kitchen where we shared a bed, my desire to play on the elder Kowalskis' piano as often as possible spurred me on to making great strides in my musical development, and to improving my playing ability. I loved the sound of the instrument and 'drank' thirstily every phrase of music I played. As I said before, my 'teacher' at the time was not very skilled, as she herself readily admitted.

My experience with her was unlike the real piano lessons I had received, alas for a short time, just before the war broke out. However, I went on eagerly from one piece of music to the next, playing anything that was available. As it happened I went through an entire album of piano transcriptions of Johann Strauss's waltzes, then various other pieces, none of which would have been given to me to play by a professional teacher. Yet today, as a concert pianist, I am convinced that I owe a great debt to that unorthodox, but invaluable experience of piano playing in childhood. I was left free to have really spontaneous encounters with the music and the instrument, unfettered by overly restrictive 'guidance'. My undiluted joy of the music I played was fresh and totally spontaneous. In these encounters with music lay deeply rooted needs from which my musical talent later blossomed.

The fate that landed us in little Pruszków, diverting us from what was to be the end of our lives (that is, our journey to Auschwitz) did not see the end of my piano playing. On the contrary — living and hiding during the SS raids in our crowded little converted pigsty, my ear caught the sound of a piano from a neighbouring house. I used to stop outside that house and listen to those sounds. Once again, I began trying to persuade my mother to approach the people who lived in the house and ask if I could be allowed to play their piano sometime. Mother relented and one day went to speak to the neighbour who, it transpired, was the village piano teacher, and who gave lessons to youngsters from the surrounding area. She allotted a special time for me, when she did not have to teach, so that I could come and play her piano for half an hour each day.

On one of these occasions, shortly after I started practising in the neighbour's house, she came into the room to
listen to me play, and then began to give me some instruction. Within two or three weeks she approached my mother
saying that I had real musical talent and ought to have more
opportunities to play than she was able to offer me She
therefore contacted a woman (Mrs M.) who lived in the same
street and arranged for me to practise every day on her piano.
Mrs M. was a wealthy widow and lived alone. She received
me with great kindness and generosity. I was free to come
and play her piano as often as I wanted. Within days of
our meeting she began to invite me to eat with her, obviously realising how poor we were. In those days, we were
truly penniless.

Our contact with Uncle Max, who used to support us
financially, was lost. We did not know his whereabouts.
Mother found a means of earning by making home-made
cigarettes through the night and selling them on a street
corner during the day. Cigarettes were in short supply but
one could make them using some kind of tobacco and a little
handheld gadget for stuffing the tobacco into empty cigarette
filters. Mother and I used to go out with anything between 20
and 100 of these home-made filter cigarettes, lay them neatly
on a piece of old newspaper on the pavement and sell them
to passers-by a few at a time. This brought in some pennies
of income which we could use to buy bread and other basic
foods to sustain us.

Those months we spent in our tiny place in Pruszków, living together with Mrs Topolska and her two daughters, took
on a certain pattern for my mother and me. We sat up at night

filling the cigarette filters with tobacco. Mother went on late into the night, having sent me off to sleep earlier. Once again, as in the apartment of the Kowalski family, we had to share one bed which had only a thin mattress. The two other beds in our little place were shared between the three Topolski women. We were all truly poor and only able to earn just enough for meagre food. However, our cigarette 'business' became quite successful; we started selling all the cigarettes we displayed on our little corner of the village street. We attracted a regular clientele. The same customers would stop by each day, have a little chat with Mother and me, and buy their few cigarettes.

Business went so well that one day, after a successful sales session, Mother took me to the local shop and, her face beaming with pleasure, treated me to a large glass of milk and a crusty roll with fresh ham – a true luxury in those days. I often remember that moment and the expression on my mother's face as she watched me hungrily eating my 'special treat'. To a woman who so strictly adhered to Jewish traditions, it would have been unthinkable in any other circumstances and in any other times for her to allow her child to eat ham. Yet at that time she must have decided that no religious law should stand in the way of a mother nourishing a hungry child.

The cigarette business went on and even grew during the late autumn and winter of 1944 and early spring of 1945. Mother was advised to produce boxes of a few hundred cigarettes and sell them wholesale to local kiosks and shops. That meant sitting through almost the entire night filling several hundred filters with tobacco.

I remember one rather extraordinary thing about that period – the last months before Hitler's defeat. There was a quiet German soldier, probably in his late thirties, in a Wehrmacht uniform, who must have spotted Mother selling her cigarettes in the street. One day he accompanied us back to our little home. Mother was worried and embarrassed. She had to invite him in. From then on, he used to visit almost every evening, and sit drinking tea and watching Mother work at her cigarette-making. He had obviously fallen in love with her. And she had to be extremely gentle and careful not to cause any trouble. Luckily, she managed to confine their relationship to his visiting us in our tiny improvised home where she had not only me there, but also Mrs Topolska and her daughters. Naturally he never guessed that we were Jewish; he must have felt lonely and missed feminine warmth and children's company. We were constantly marvelling at the fact that he so devotedly kept paying his evening calls at our pigsty, often bringing what treats he could. Mother dared not hide her knowledge of German from him so they could sit and chat for hours. The poor man came from a small place in Germany, missed his home and felt terribly alone in this country where almost no one spoke any German (except for the Jews, who by then were nowhere to be found), and where no one had anything but hateful feelings for his countrymen.

CHAPTER 10

The Last Winter of the War

We seemed to have packed a great many experiences into less than a year between the Warsaw Uprising and the eventual expulsion of the Germans from Poland at the end of the war in Europe in May 1945.

We continued to live and, on many occasions, hide from sudden SS raids, in our makeshift home. Mother went on earning a little money through her cigarette sales. I helped her and went with her to places where she sold them. I also went every day to Mrs M's house to practise the piano and she always insisted on giving me lunch. One day she announced that she had arranged for a piano teacher to come once a week to give her lessons. She had decided it would be nice to learn to play again. She added that while the teacher was there I 'might just as well also have a lesson'. Her delicacy in offering charity was remarkable. . . Needless to say, I loved having lessons and being guided through new, unfamiliar music. I think that these oases of inner fulfilment must have meant more than I realised in keeping me sane under the harassing circumstances of everything else in our lives at that time. I loved music and I loved the piano. Every new piece I learned to play (although again under the guidance of a pretty uninspired teacher), gave me enormous pleasure and a great sense of excitement.

Throughout the war years my main attention was focused on all that was happening around us which threatened to destroy our lives, yet somewhere within me there always remained that deep passion for music. I never wanted to be anything other than a pianist. Somehow, amidst the most impossible and unlikely situations, that desire stayed alive and brought about my repeated contact with the piano in most unexpected ways.

Mrs M. must have sensed my inner urgency, added to which the person who had introduced me to her had spoken to her about my musical gifts. This made her decide to help me in every way she could. That meant not only letting me come to her home to practise, then getting a teacher for me under the pretext of taking lessons herself, but also helping with the necessities of life like food and clothes. Yes, clothes as well. We really had absolutely no possessions when we found ourselves in the village. A few secondhand things were given to us immediately on our arrival but, with winter drawing nearer, we did not have any adequate clothing for the severity of cold which one could expect in Poland.

One day when I came to practise at Mrs M's home she met me with a smile and announced that she would take me to her shoemaker, who was preparing special warm winter boots for her. 'It so happens' she said, 'that there is a lot of spare material [thick woollen felt and leather, which I clearly remember] so he might as well make a pair each for you and your mother'. This was true kindness and generosity. We could not have survived the Polish winter in our thin shoes without getting severe frostbite which could have led to lots of other complications. Mrs M. realised that we could not possibly have the money to buy winter boots, essential items of winter clothing in the snow and frost. We were deeply touched and grateful. That winter was made easier for us by this gentle woman's kindness At least a lack of proper footwear was not one of the discomforts we endured that winter. Our little hut was dark, having only one tiny window, but this was possibly a blessing in disguise for us, as the raiding SS men never guessed we hid there. It was also damp and it had no toilet; that was outside in the yard. I don't mention a bathroom since that word had long since left our vocabulary. We used to heat water in a bucket over the primus stove and invented ingenious forms of 'showering', which involved standing in a large metal bowl and pouring jugs of warm water over our shivering bodies to get clean. All this did not seem too much trouble to us. We could at least be clean and, after all, we were alive. In those days surviving and remaining unharmed was our primary concern, aim and task. Our hope was for Mother's prayer to be answered, 'Lord protect me and help me to survive these times without anything but my daughters unharmed'; I used to hear her say this often.

That last winter of the war saw us managing somehow. Mother's cigarette sales continued and our business grew. However, we were no longer standing in the streets, but selling wholesale to a few shops and kiosks. We considered ourselves very lucky to be able to earn our modest living

that way since we had no other income at all. Mrs Kowalska
with her baby girl and the little boy Jacek went their separate
ways after we were released from the Auschwitz train. Her
husband had disappeared with the resistance fighters and
when we last saw her she did not know if he was alive or
not. We knew nothing of Uncle Max's whereabouts, so his
help was not available. We had no way of finding out what
had happened to him and his close family – his wife and son,
as well as his mother-in-law and sister-in-law – during the
fighting and subsequent destruction of Warsaw. The Nazis
had systematically destroyed, with ruthless deliberation,
every street and house in Warsaw. The city was turned to
ashes. Not one building remained standing. It looked like the
ghost of a once lively and beautiful place.

All this was happening in the sixth year of the war and it
was our privilege and good fortune to have survived so far,
in spite of almost insurmountable difficulties and dangers.
We were worn out by all the ordeals – perhaps, I should
say, my mother in particular. I kept going with the amazing resilience of a child. I experienced painful anxiety and
fears, but somewhere within me was a constant deep trust
that we would survive it all. On occasions when danger grew
and hope diminished I prayed. I did so with great intensity,
then hope and trust were renewed. My prayers were highly
unstudied. I can hardly describe them – they were an inner
call for survival.

One undeniable fact supported the rumours that the
Russians would come to the aid of the resistance fighters,
namely the continued presence of the Red Army on the east
bank of the River Vistula. But the Russian forces stayed in that

part of Warsaw throughout the fighting of the resistance and did not march in to stop the Germans murdering thousands of civilians and destroying the main part of the city. There were feelings of bitterness and despair at the fact that such a mighty army had stood still, waiting to come into central Warsaw after its funeral, as it were. There must have been ulterior political reasons for them to do so. For us, however, it was inexplicable that we were not rescued from the Nazi oppression for almost a whole year. In those circumstances, for some of us, each day and night under Nazi occupation meant a toss-up between life and death.

In the last months before our liberation, when we discovered where my sister was, we heard of an extraordinary thing she had done one day. Through similar experiences to ours she had got out of Warsaw and found shelter in a village outside the city, where she worked as a domestic help. She was not too far away from us, although for some months we did not know where she was or even whether she was alive.

One day, as my sister walked in the street, a worn-out, shabbily dressed young man approached her, looked at her and without hesitation said, 'Please can you help me, I am a survivor of the Warsaw ghetto. I have been hiding in the city sewers and have just emerged. I have not eaten for a long time and have nowhere to go, nowhere to hide any more. . . please can you help me?' She was shaken and horrified at his pitiful state, but also frightened. However, without considering the danger, she decided on a desperate and risky course of action. Her response to the plea of the desperate young Jewish man was to take him immediately to the little local hospital where she had recently been recovering from scarlet fever, which she contracted after getting out of Warsaw. She was a lovely and lively 18-year-old at the time and became very friendly with the nurses and doctors while staying at the hospital, so she persuaded the nurses to admit the man as a patient. They were told the truth about his identity, which meant that in keeping him on a ward as a fake patient they were endangering their own lives. Anyone finding a Jew alive was still expected to hand them over to the Nazi authorities, and there were severe penalties for harbouring Jews. Thus, the fugitive was saved not only from the threat of being captured and executed, but also from the sickness and starvation which awaited him. He did, in fact, survive the war although my sister knew that there were a few hair-raising moments when Nazis came to inspect the hospital and he had to pretend to be almost unconscious in his bed. Had they for some reason asked to examine the male patients (as they often did in various circumstances) and seen him as a circumcised Jew, they would not only have killed him, but all the nurses and doctors protecting him. How mad, how insane can be the conditioning of the human mind which accepts such an 'ideology' as its guiding light! Where does the notion that being born a Jew is a punishable crime come from?

It was indeed much harder, almost impossible, for Jewish males to hide their identity successfully, than it was for some women, for obvious reasons. In Poland, no Christian males were ever circumcised – that ritual was only performed by the Jews. Consequently, whenever any male fell into the hands of the Gestapo, a look at his anatomy would provide indisputable proof of his Jewish origin.

I learned after the war that my Uncle Max had actually been denounced once to the Gestapo. They arrested him but, incredibly enough, even though they undressed him and saw he was circumcised, they let themselves be persuaded by an elaborate story he told them about his being circumcised because of some special genital disease he had. His otherwise non-Semitic looks and very good false documents were a strong support in his favour, and he was released! However, such miraculous escapes from death were very rare in those days – and Uncle Max was both uncommonly brave at that moment and very lucky. These Nazis were not only brutal but also very often downright stupid.

CHAPTER 11

The End of Nazi Occupation

We spent the winter of 1944–45 with Mrs Topolska and her two daughters in our little pigsty home. It was damp and often cold. We had only very basic clothes apart from our marvellous handmade boots, as mentioned, provided by Mrs M's shoemaker. We survived.

The spring came and there was a vague feeling of hope in the atmosphere. It became increasingly evident that the Russians were preparing to mount an all-out offensive against the Germans in the Warsaw area and other parts of Poland. We waited, prayed and hoped.

When we began to hear the sound of gun fire it was sweet music to our ears. After more than five years of persecution, deprivation and fear we almost did not dare to hope that we might be liberated from it all. We began to notice signs that all was not well with the German forces. They were planting landmines and destroying important bridges, roads and strategic sites, thus showing that they were obviously losing the war and were preparing to withdraw from Poland. News of the offensive on the Western front would occasionally reach us from the BBC's overseas broadcasts, received in secret. There was an air of anticipation of a major historic change in the fate of Europe and we all began to sense it.

However, our grim and frightening day-to-day reality still went on. We continued to be watchful in case the SS were still trying to capture Warsaw's survivors. We continued to live in fear and uncertainty.

In the spring of 1945 the sounds of battle became more frequent and more intensive. We saw troops on the move. Finally, the long hoped for, but almost unbelievable, day came. Someone knocked on the door of our little place, rushed in and elatedly shouted out: 'They are gone! Mrs Zachaczewska, the Germans are gone!! Come out into the streets and see for yourself!'

My mother stood completely still for some time. She was stunned. The news was almost more than she could take in. She could not react for a while. Then, still as if in a hypnotic state of awe, she took me by the hand and walked with me into the main street of the village. The scene there was one of elation and disbelief. People were laughing, crying, embracing each other and cheering the soldiers of the Soviet Red Army as they drove along slowly in their tanks, waving to the crowds. A profusion of flowers was thrown on to the tanks. The Polish people were greeting their liberators! And we Jews (the few who had reached that moment alive, though in disguise) were almost unable to comprehend the enormity of the change in our situation. We were dazed, not knowing how to respond – it seemed more than we were ready to experience. Freedom! What was the meaning of that word? No more hiding, lying, or escaping. All of that had vanished overnight with the fleeing Nazis. My mother cried as she stood there amongst the cheering, exultant crowds.

Gradually, a few individuals in the crowd began cautiously looking around and asking others 'Are you one, too. . . ?' or '*Amchu? Amchu?*' These were Jews like us who had survived in different extraordinary ways. Soon, once the war was over, vast campaigns were mounted to trace surviving relatives. Alas, most were never found and their fate remained only guessed at.

Immediately after our liberation from Nazi occupation, we contacted my sister and asked her to join us, so that the three of us could try to re-establish some sort of family life together. She, however, felt unable to leave the house in which she worked as a domestic help because the young couple who employed her had just had their first baby and badly needed her assistance. We had to wait for our reunion. Meanwhile Mother searched for other relatives and to our great joy discovered that her dear brother, Uncle Max, was alive and well, together with his family. He had managed to get out of the burning city of Warsaw and later went to Łódz in western Poland. He urged Mother to take me there and try to settle in that town. It was there that I finally went to a music school where a great fuss was made of my musical gifts. Łódz was, incidentally, the birthplace of one of the twentieth century's great pianists – Arthur Rubinstein.

CHAPTER 12

Liberation – Beginnings of a New Life

In the early days after our liberation an extraordinary incident occurred which resolved for my sister Jasia a painful question which had been on her mind. As soon as it was possible to get through the ruins, small groups of people made their way through Warsaw's destroyed streets to search for remnants of their homes and possessions. Jasia went with such a group one day and found the ashes of what used to be the Kowalskis' house in Trembacka Street in the centre of Warsaw, where Mother and I had last lived. The large apartment house had been reduced to a burnt-out shell, as had all the others in Warsaw. However, the cellars had remained intact, buried under the debris, and Jasia and her companions managed to dig down into the cellar beneath the Kowalskis' building. There she found a small suitcase, which she recognised as ours, and which contained a few of our personal belongings. Mother had taken some things down to the cellar at the outset of the uprising in case we had to stay there for any length of time.

Jasia brought the suitcase back to our village, and when she gave it to my mother, who immediately opened it to see what was there, she spotted an old envelope in it. 'What is this?' she exclaimed. 'It looks like Poldi's writing.' Before Mother could even react, she had opened the envelope and found Poldi's last letter to her, in which he broke off their engagement. It was the very letter – and the only one – which Mother had kept from Jasia. And now it had found its way to her in the most bizarre circumstances. Needless to say, she received a great shock on reading it and felt deeply hurt that Mother had hidden it from her. Only after much persuasion did she accept that Mother had acted only out of concern for her by protecting her from yet another harrowing experience.

At the time Jasia discovered the letter we had absolutely no way of finding out what had happened to Dr Poldi. Mother thought that perhaps he had married the Polish nurse with whom he shared a house – there may have been a moral obligation for him to do so. It was some two years after the war ended that he unexpectedly contacted us. He was on his way to a Swiss sanatorium and met us briefly. It was then that the true reason for his writing that dramatic letter during the war came to light. A little while after my sister left Lwów for Warsaw Poldi was diagnosed with tuberculosis. At that time, there was no cure for the illness, which was highly contagious and often fatal. So, out of deep concern and love for my sister, he decided to break off their engagement. After our meeting, Poldi continued on his way to Switzerland. My sister stayed in Poland for a few more years. Their paths diverged completely.

Many years later, while living with her family in Australia, Jasia discovered that Dr Poldi had in fact recovered in Switzerland and later emigrated to Sydney where he worked as a psychiatrist. He was married to a fellow doctor whom he had met during his convalescence in Switzerland. My sister and Dr Poldi met again on several occasions in Australia. She always kept a very special feeling for this man who had meant so much to her at such a vital and dramatic time in her youth. All of us, in fact, felt an affection for, and gratitude to Dr Poldi, that extraordinarily gifted, courageous, resourceful and unselfish man. We owed our survival, in large measure, to him.

The dark, terrible years of war over, we had to find our way back to normal life. Our task of escaping death at the hands of the Nazis was at an end. Now it was necessary to find a home, a means of earning our living and, for me at least, to enter school and give my whole attention to what I had always wanted to do – become a musician, a concert pianist.

This desire had not been dimmed, even by all that we had endured and witnessed in those frightening years of war. But now I could really plunge into learning and playing, and my thirst for both was very great. After we found Mother's brother, Uncle Max, alive and unharmed, he set out to help my mother find a home, and she began work in an office. Her days as a maid were over. She no longer had to play the role of a simple, uneducated countrywoman. At last she could be her natural self again. She found her work satisfying, and was able to support me in every way so that I could devote my time entirely to my studies.

I realise that, in this account of my life, the theme of anti-Semitism in Poland – which I often witnessed – appears a number of times. However, I must also acknowledge the kindness and courage of those Polish Christians, aware of the tragedy of our plight, who often risked their lives to help us Jews to escape the Nazi persecution. Many such people are commemorated on the Jerusalem memorial to 'The Righteous Among the Nations', and it is thanks to them that we survived.

For me, this has mitigated my reaction to the senseless anti-Semitism I encountered, and kept alive my warm feelings for the country of my birth, its people, music, landscape and culture. It has enabled me, in recent years, to accept invitations to be a guest teacher there. I have given masterclasses working with piano students as well as teachers, and given introductions at workshops on a subject hitherto unknown in Poland: the Alexander Technique applied to piano playing. Each such visit to Poland has provided a truly moving contact with my past.

Part II

POLAND 1945–50

CHAPTER 13

Fulfilment Through Learning

Between May 1945 and May 1950, I gave all my energies to learning everything I was offered at school but especially to working on my piano playing, which I did with great passion.

The war over, with Poland largely destroyed and wounded as a country, the process began to re-establish a normal life for its people. The city of Warsaw, before the war Poland's cultural centre as well as its capital, lay in ruins. The Nazis had turned a city of some one and a half million inhabitants to ashes; there was not a single building intact or habitable. Everything was shattered and burnt. The Jewish ghetto, of course, had already been savagely destroyed some two years earlier and almost all of its inhabitants killed. The non-Jewish population of Warsaw also suffered much at the hands of the Nazis, but those who survived the uprising and its tragic consequences began to move back into the city and rebuild their lives. Eminent Polish intellectuals and artists, former citizens of Warsaw but now dispersed to other parts of the country, began speedily and eagerly to return to their respective fields of work. Schools, universities, music and art colleges were gradually re-established. Post-war Poland was now under Soviet influence. Many new institutions were created, modelled on their Russian counterparts, and so in the field of musical education new systems were established.

In Katowice – a centre for heavy industry in south-west Poland – the very first Music High School for gifted young musicians (the Liceum Muzyczne) was opened with some of the outstanding teachers who could not, at that point, return to Warsaw. The School offered a broad spectrum of secondary education but accepted only pupils who showed musical talent of the kind which carried the promise of a professional future in music. Although I had missed out on attending primary school and had only received a rudimentary education at home, I was sent for an entrance examination to this prestigious school. I had to sit a written test, answer an aural one and, of course, play for a music audition. To our great joy the School accepted me without reservation, though I doubt that my academic achievements at that point won the place for me. I have good reason to believe that it was my musical talent which brought me into that school, in spite of its select choice of students. From the moment I began to study at the Liceum Muzyczne my real life as a musician was initiated. There I began my true musical education from very fine teachers, who ranked amongst the best in the long-established and excellent tradition of Polish musicians, particularly pianists.

There was a curious coincidence in my preparation for the entrance exam in Katowice. Not having been to a formal

1. Grandfather
   Isidor Linden
   – Mother's father

2. Grandmother
   Leah Helen Linden
   – Mother's mother

3. Nelly aged 4 with her parents and sister on holiday before the war

4. L-R, Mother, Nelly and Alicja Topolska in Warsaw during the war

5. Nelly with Zygmunt Topolski and, on the left, Alicja and
Mrs Topolska, Mother and Jola in Warsaw during the war

6. The destruction of Warsaw during World War II

7. Sister Janette, in 1946

8. Mother, in 1946

9. Nelly with her sister and mother shortly after the end of the war

10. Janette and her husband Julian

11. Nelly at the Mozart Piano Competition, Israel 1952

12. Receiving first prize in Mozart Piano Competition
from Claudio Arrau

13. Henrietta Michaelson, Nelly's piano teacher in Jerusalem

14. The Dalet Kleir Shir quartet

15. Nelly and Roger's wedding, Kensington Register Office

16. Nelly at the piano, mid 1960s

17. Nelly and Roger with baby Daniela

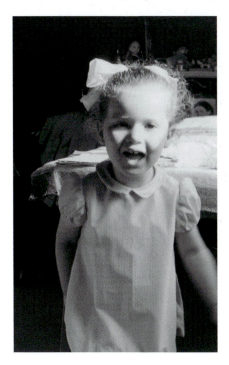

18. Young Daniela

19. Nelly, Daniela (aged 5) with Uncle Max and his wife in New York

20. Patrick Macdonald,
    Nelly's teacher of the
    Alexander Technique

21. Nelly and Mother in England, 1970

22. Nelly and Roger in Oxford, 1970s

23. Roger shortly before retirement, 1986

24. Daniela portrait, 2015

25. Daniela singing at Pizza Express Jazz Club, 2013

26. Nelly giving a
masterclass in
her studio

27. Nelly performing, 2015

school during the war, I was totally unsure of myself in terms of sitting the entrance exam, and quite ignorant of what might be expected of me. The night before my test I remember asking my sister and her new boyfriend, Julian, to prepare me for next day's ordeal. They both seriously and quickly tried to cram into me some bits of useful information, paying particular attention to my knowledge of arithmetic and teaching me an instant version of fractions. To my relief and amazement these were the very questions I was asked in the exam and I was, therefore, able to give the correct answers; absolute chance helped me through that problem.

Within a year at that fine school, I began to lead my own class in all subjects and came into the privileged group of the most musically gifted pupils, who were chosen from among the whole school on different occasions to appear in public performances. In a sense that was the beginning of my life as a concert pianist. After initially placing me with a young teacher, the school soon transferred me to one of the senior instructors. Her name was Wanda Chmielowska who, in her youth, was taught by the renowned Russian pianist Annette Essipowa. Wanda mainly taught the most advanced students on what would be considered a postgraduate level. My thirst for learning and playing was almost unquenchable. In every subject at school I was either the best or one of the best in my year. There was so much I was absorbing from the wide range of subjects we all had to study. These included maths, physics, chemistry, geography, history (modern and ancient), Polish and European literature, Latin and modern languages, as well as a number of specialised music subjects. Everything interested me and I spent most of my time after school doing my homework, practising the piano and reading.

Looking back at those first years after the war it seems as if my voracious appetite for academic and musical progress was partly a reaction to the years of repression, fear and deprivation of every kind that I had experienced previously. It was as if the darkness of the war years had been lifted, and the bright light and fresh air of freedom filled my whole being with a need to receive as much as possible of all I had missed before. Just as a person starved of food over a long period of time might react greedily to being given unlimited amounts of food, so I was responding to those new opportunities of learning and developing my musical gifts with utmost enthusiasm. Whereas a child who grew up in normal circumstances, and not in such abnormal, dangerous and terrible times as I did, might, as a teenager, react against all forms of discipline, I eagerly accepted and, indeed, imposed on myself the discipline required for such intensive learning.

Yet, not surprisingly, some loophole in this attitude of almost excessive seriousness in my early teens appeared occasionally in silly irrational behaviour.

Within the first years at my school I became known as a soloist and at the age of about 13 was chosen from amongst some 300 pupils to perform in a big public concert the school put on at the city's Philharmonic Hall. Also taking part were the school symphony orchestra, a mixed chorus and a few other soloists. (Over 30 years later I discovered amongst my mother's well-kept memorabilia a review in the regional Polish paper referring to my playing on that occasion.) There were other events in which I was chosen to play, a fact which gave me a somewhat privileged status at the school. The fact that I was also collecting prizes for general progress in learning prompted the director of the school to award me a special scholarship – the 'Chopin Stypendium'.

Somehow the balancing act between this excellence and the nature of teenage behaviour, as well as my reaction to the war, brought to the surface unexpected outbursts of apparently unreasonable aggression. This found its target in one of the kindest and least assertive of our teachers, the Latin master; during a number of lessons, he was on the receiving end of old slippers and pieces of fruit which were thrown at him seemingly 'from nowhere'. I placed myself at the very back of the class on these occasions (normally I was in the first row of desks) and with great glee mischievously flung things at the unsuspecting, kind man during his enthusiastic exposition of some Latin text. The climax of these bouts of irrational aggression came when I was identified as the culprit responsible for the disrupted lessons, and the school's director (the equivalent of an English headmaster) called me into his office. There the man looked almost embarrassed at having to face me as one accused of such strange senseless behaviour, rather than the much praised and prize-winning pupil. He reprimanded me severely. My mother was going to be notified of this shameful behaviour of her daughter. . . the prestigious Chopin scholarship was to be withdrawn from me. I think the shock of this interview helped me out of that episode of unruly behaviour. My mother was very depressed at discovering that her cherished daughter had displayed such an apparently delinquent side of herself.

The whole thing blew over within about a month, my scholarship was reinstated and I continued my education as before. It seems as if, having absorbed so much of the aggression around me during the war and having had to control and suppress most of my feelings while hiding, escaping and trying to stay alive, some misplaced anger surfaced in this irrational demonstration of uncontrolled behaviour. Something in me simply could not stand being good the whole time. There had to be another side to me which needed to be acknowledged.

CHAPTER 14

New Influences – Literature

On the whole, our lives in the years between 1945 and 1950 were very industrious and, for me particularly, highly creative. I lived with my mother and her youngest sister Marysia, who had miraculously survived her own ordeal during the Nazi occupation. The local authority in Katowice gave us a minute, dark apartment consisting of a kitchen and one other room. There was no bathroom, and the only toilet opposite our little flat across an inner courtyard of the building was shared by us and a neighbour living on a floor below. On bath days, we warmed buckets of water on the stove and washed in a large laundry tub in the kitchen. It was quite a complicated procedure, yet in those days nothing seemed to give us cause for complaint or self-pity. Our memories of previous experiences were so vivid that some physical discomfort did not seem to be a serious reason to be worried or irritated by. We felt so privileged and grateful to be alive. Any difficulties we encountered in our daily lives after the war were nothing compared with living under constant threat to our freedom, our basic human dignity and our very existence. Once we arrived in Katowice and I started attending the music school, Mother took up a post in the office of the Ministry of Health. Her warm personality and willingness to spare no effort in her work won her both appreciation and friends among her colleagues. In those days, she did all she could to enable me to devote my entire time to studying. This could not have been too easy, as she had to work full time and be responsible for running our modest household. Auntie Marysia was always very kind and helpful, while I did my share of duties by looking after my own things, but really everything that was not related to my music school studies or literature seemed to me to be an unnecessary, burdensome chore.

My days were filled with what I loved best: encounters with music, literature and poetry; learning about past and present human endeavours and achievements; becoming acquainted with stories of the lives and times of great men of music; and learning about heroes of modern and ancient history, as well as writers – Polish, French, Russian and English.

One day I noticed a bundle of old books stored on top of an old cupboard in our room. They had been abandoned there by whoever had lived in the place before us. I took the books down and saw an unusual, unreadable name of an author who was certainly not Polish. The books seemed to be all dialogues between different characters with names that were more or less unpronounceable in Polish. I started reading the first one and became absolutely absorbed in it from the very beginning. I could not put it down. With great fascination, I went on reading the dramatic story of a king who divides his kingdom between two of his daughters, while disinheriting the third who does not flaunt her true affection for him; only later does she prove her devotion and loyalty to her distressed father. The king's name – Lear – was strange to me. I did not know where the plot took place and, as for the author, his curious name (Shakespeare) meant nothing to me. Of course, I had heard people mention the great 'Szekspir', but I had no idea that the wonderful plays I had accidently discovered and was reading so excitedly – *King Lear, Hamlet, Macbeth, A Midsummer Night's Dream*, all translated into Polish – were in any way related to the famous 'Szekspir'. The identity of the creator of some of the world's greatest writing was, unsurprisingly, not known then to the young ignorant girl in Poland.

My life in those post-war days was full of wonder and emotional excitement. I began to form strong friendships with other young people around me. The more sophisticated, philosophically inclined and artistically endowed they were, the more I felt drawn to them. One such young girl, Barbara Bielinska, became my closest friend. She was the only child of a highly cultured couple who introduced their daughter from an early age to the finest European literature, and guided her towards developing a discriminating taste in art and literature. Barbara and I became inseparable. She got into our school, strangely enough, not on the strength of her musical gifts, which were pretty average, but most probably because of her exceptional intelligence, erudition (which was way above that of her contemporaries) and her general artistic inclinations. She eventually became a highly successful painter and graphic artist. For me Barbara and her parents became a source of education and, through them, I discovered far more about art and literature than I would have done through school or from my mother. Above all, perhaps, our friendship provided the opportunity for us to share all the intense feelings and ideas which were arising in our young hearts and minds. We could share our innermost secrets which we felt neither her parents nor my mother could be let into. However, there was one thing I kept hidden from everyone around me, even Barbara, and that was my real identity.

My mother and I still retained our wartime false names and all the documents that went with them. Indeed, we had no papers stating our true pre-war names and other particulars, but the reason for not declaring who we really were lay in the dark depths of our fear and mistrust of the society around us: a sad psychological consequence of the Holocaust. Having hidden the truth about our being Jewish for such a long time, it was easier to continue using our assumed, Christian-sounding and absolutely Polish, name of Zachaczewska even when the persecution of Jews was over. There were a number of Jewish people who had managed to escape death with the help of false papers, as we did, but who in the post-war years still went under their assumed names and did not disclose their Jewish identity to anyone. Many Jewish people still felt endangered by the residual undercurrents of Polish anti-Semitism. Of course, the truth is that in a society with such a long history of strong anti-Semitism, even Hitler's outrages did not uproot the tradition of animosity towards the Jews. However, our shying away from openly announcing who we really were had much to do with the extent of our identity anxiety, brought about by our experiences of Nazism.

I therefore began to give my first public concerts, under the aegis of the school, as Aniela Zachaczewska. Officially, no one at my school knew that I was Jewish, nor did they know the truth about my family's experiences during the war. I do believe, however, that several of my friends at school guessed that we were not really Christians. Once even Barbara, in spite of her real affection for me, said in a moment of sarcasm, 'Well every Jew is now called Podolski or Kowalski' – typically pure Polish, non-Jewish names. Yet my own piano teacher, Mme Chmielowska, one of Poland's foremost piano teachers, who had great affection for me and great hopes for my future as a pianist, seemed to accept my false identity without question. This became quite obvious to me when one day, commenting on the playing of a remarkable child prodigy violinist whom she went to hear, she said 'He is quite wonderful, but what of it? He is regrettably a little Jew'. I remember that remark very clearly. My heart sank, I felt hurt and alienated. Wanda Chmielowska, who was then middle-aged, was someone I revered and had always looked up to with admiration and respect – but even she was prey to her nation's irrational, deep prejudice against us Jews.

I continued to maintain a kind of double existence as a person inwardly conscious of who I really was and outwardly playing the part I had been forced to adopt during the war. Something in me was endeavouring to be liberated, yet I did not question why Mother did not come out into the open about who we were. The tremendous resentment and anger against this awful prejudice simmered in my mind all the time and I knew that before too long it would have to be resolved.

Later, when we came to live in Israel, our first chance for a liberation from that oppressive feeling was a wonderful new reality. Yet now, after so much more time and so many more life experiences, I realise that I, for one, have really never become totally free from the effects of such extreme anti-Semitism. To this day, when in a public place in England (which is now my home) or some other country, I will hide from view the title of a book on a Jewish subject, or hide the name of a Jewish newspaper. I notice myself doing this often quite automatically; otherwise there arises somewhere in me still an inexplicable feeling of awkwardness, the freedom of my present surroundings notwithstanding.

My schooldays in Katowice brought with them much excitement and, often, magic into my life. My continued relationship with music played a large part in this. But there was much else which enriched that period of my life: my friendship with Barbara gave both of us the opportunity to share all the immensely passionate experiences of our youth. Of course, falling desperately in love with an unattainable person, whether from the cinema screen or someone else quite beyond my reach, gave rise to flights of fancy and an outpouring of feelings that provided material for so many youthful dreams. For a time, one object of my adolescent amorous crushes was the strikingly impressive English actor James Mason, who appeared in the film *The Seventh Veil*, in which Ann Todd played the dramatic role of a concert pianist. What a potent association for a budding pianist!

Sadly, there were other dreams too, which assailed my nights. The richer, more creative and fulfilling my life became, the more it was overshadowed by a threatening darkness of dreams and nightmares about the war, as if they came each night demanding my attention. Life for me became split between days of brightness with creative action and hopes for an exciting musical future, and nights disturbed by a world of dreams representing vividly haunting scenes in which I was being chased by the SS, held at gunpoint, and about to be executed; I would wake up in a cold sweat, shouting for help. That became the regular pattern of my nights which was to last for years to come. My great zeal for learning and achieving as much as I could helped, to an extent, to camouflage the states of anxiety which found their regular expression mainly in those frightening dreams.

I did so well in my studies, and made such great strides in my musical development that within two years my teacher decided that I should give my first full length public recital in the Music School's concert hall. The recital was a great success. Wanda Chmielowska, my distinguished piano teacher at the time, later admitted that she had had to resist the temptation to take me to other major cities in Poland to 'show me off' as a young pianist prodigy. She felt that, although it would make me well known and enhance her reputation as a teacher, I needed to live a normal life, and to continue both my musical and general development undisturbed.

Naturally, success tasted sweet and gave me further encouragement and the impetus to work hard. I spent most of my time practising, reading, doing homework and going to concerts and to the local opera house. In that early postwar period, as a result of the total destruction of Warsaw, Katowice became the home of some of Poland's most accomplished musicians. We youngsters in Katowice, therefore, had a unique opportunity to hear the best concerts given by the symphony orchestra, the radio orchestra and some of the finest soloists. All this not only added to the excitement of our musical lives but provided a rich foundation for a well-rounded musical education – quite a privileged situation in a country so severely afflicted by the war and barely beginning to recover from its destruction. The pupils of the Music Liceum had free passes to all musical events: on showing our school identity card we could enter any concert or opera performance and either have a standing place or take any unoccupied seat. In this way, by my mid-teens I was acquainted with much of the symphonic music and various works for different instruments with orchestra. I heard my first *Carmen, Aida, Madame Butterfly, Rigoletto, Figaro, The Barber of Seville, Halka* (a national Polish opera by Moniuszko) and much else. At school, there were many concerts given by various students and student ensembles. I particularly enjoyed singing in our choir which numbered almost 300; all pupils were obliged to participate in its regular rehearsals and to sing in concerts.

I discovered another small outlet for my performing inclinations when I was asked to take part in special children's programmes on the radio. It seemed that my voice and diction came across very well over the microphone and, what's more, I took to acting in little sketches with great enthusiasm. Strangely, performing as a radio actress never made me nervous, quite unlike performing as a pianist – even at that young age. When I gave my first recital at the age of 13, I can well remember how sick with nerves I felt the whole day leading up to the performance. Once on the stage, however, some magic took over and the excitement of music-making overcame the nerves. Being extremely nervous prior to public performances has never diminished for me – if anything it has become more intense over the years.

As well as the Chopin scholarship, I had a piano given to me by the government authorities. This was, of course, my most precious and indispensable possession. Though our living conditions were very frugal – the kitchen and room we lived in had one window each, letting in limited daylight from a completely walled-in courtyard – I spent hours at my piano. Sometimes Mother even tried to suggest that I should go to some school party or outing, but I willingly missed them in favour of staying at home to play.

CHAPTER 15

Jasia and Julian

During this period my sister, Jasia, was living in another city where she had moved with her young husband, Julian. She undertook to study medicine and was doing extremely well. She also sang a lot and had singing lessons to further develop her fine lyrical soprano voice. I have been told that our father had a good voice and passionately loved opera. No doubt my sister's singing gifts were inherited from Father's side of the family. Her marriage to Julian had an unusual background and beginning. In the first few weeks after the war Jasia met her future husband when he, a young Polish soldier attached to the Red Army, came to the apartment in which she lived as domestic help to a young couple. Julian knocked at the door; Jasia opened it. He announced that he had army orders to take over a room in the apartment for his commanding officer. They looked at each other: she, a beautiful young girl with large black eyes, dark curled hair and a disarming smile, and he, an extremely attractive young man of barely 20, with large black eyes, dark hair and a curiously yellow complexion. Jasia explained that the apartment consisted of only one room and a kitchen and that the young couple had just become parents to their first baby. There simply was no room to accommodate anyone else. In fact, she, Jasia, was also in need of accommodation for herself. Julian smiled and suggested that she join him in his military vehicle in search of a place for herself and for his officer. She went downstairs with him. They looked at each other questioningly and understood that they were both lucky Jewish survivors of the Holocaust. From that moment, they stayed together and before too long Julian became my brother-in-law. His yellow complexion had an incredible story behind it.

Julian was the sole member of his entire close family to survive the war. At the age of 16 he, together with another boy of his age, Adam, escaped extermination in the Lublin ghetto. The two boys ran and, in the depth of night, found themselves in a village where a peasant woman rescued them; she kept them hidden in secret, not only from the entire neighbourhood but also from her own family, in a small, totally dark space under her kitchen floor. Such spaces were commonly found beneath the kitchen floors of village houses; they were used for storing winter vegetables such as potatoes, cabbages, onions and beetroots. Julian and Adam crouched in that dark space for more than seven months! Each night the woman would let them out into the kitchen, when she was certain that no one would see them. They could move around a bit and stretch their bodies. Once a day she gave them a bowl of soup and a portion of bread to keep them alive. They would spend a long time trying to cut the bread into absolutely equal halves. Had the Nazis discovered them in their hiding place, both boys would have been executed, together with all the inhabitants of the village, and the entire village would have been burned down. Fortunately, and miraculously this did not happen, but Julian and Adam, who did not see daylight for all that time, came out of hiding after Poland's liberation looking totally yellow. It took a long while for their complexions to gradually return to a normal colour.

I came to feel very affectionate towards Julian, who seemed to me very kind and friendly. Mother liked him too. Fate seemed to keep us apart, however, as Jasia and Julian lived in Wrocław, in western Poland (called Breslau under German occupation) where my sister studied medicine, while Mother and I remained in Katowice, more than a hundred miles away, until May 1950. I, therefore, enjoyed the benefits of both a general and a musical education at the splendid music school there for five years from 1945 to 1950.

During that time, there occurred the most important change in our lives since the ending of World War II. In 1948 the United Nations voted for the creation of the state of Israel. Shortly afterwards, agreements were reached for many of the survivors of the Holocaust who remained in European countries behind the 'Iron Curtain' to emigrate to Israel. Most of the surviving Jews from Poland took the opportunity to apply for an exit permit to go to Israel. The majority did go there; a few stayed in other western European countries, or elsewhere in the West.

PART III

ISRAEL 1950–60

CHAPTER 16

To the Promised Land – Israel

One day, towards the end of 1949, Mother announced that she had put our names down for a permit to emigrate to Israel. This happened a short while after the Director of my school had called me into his office to tell me that I was among the few most promising pupils chosen to be sent to the Moscow Conservatoire to continue our musical studies after matriculation at the age of 18. The Moscow Conservatoire was a mecca for all young musicians from the eastern bloc countries and was indeed a great centre of the finest tradition in piano playing. For me this was a very exciting prospect which promised to open doors to a really serious career as a pianist. Quite understandably, Mother's suggestion that we emigrate from Poland came as a shock to me. I feared the disruption of my future as a pianist, which was constantly uppermost in my hopes. This fear was further confirmed when we both visited the Israeli consular authorities and were told how basic and harsh life was in Israel, and how unlikely I was to have much chance of becoming a pianist there. However, the person dealing with our emigration papers decided to furnish me with a letter to a man called Frank Pelleg, who held the important post of head of the music department in the newly formed Ministry of Education and Culture in Israel. Frank Pelleg, originally from Prague, was also a highly respected pianist and harpsichordist.

From the day of its creation, Israel had to struggle for survival in every respect – literally defending itself from those who constantly attacked it physically in order to destroy it. Moreover, in the early fifties, the country had no viable economy capable of supporting many new immigrants. There were shortages of every kind, including food. No one starved, but there was rationing of basic foods like meat, eggs and so on. Obviously in a country having to deal with such primary necessities as survival in a very hostile region of the world, as well as with the struggle for the basic provisions of daily life, there could be little prospect for a youngster dreaming of becoming a musician, particularly someone with hardly any financial means. I was profoundly unhappy about having to leave my exciting and promising musical path to go to a country full of hardships, in which I could only expect to find work in some field other than music. Indeed, from all sides came words of warning about the difficulties of life in Israel.

We were to emigrate with just our personal belongings and a few household things; we were allowed no furniture, no larger household objects and, most painful for me, no piano. I experienced great anxiety, largely because of a deep horror of leaving our little nest. I felt frightened of losing my musical life, my friends and the freedom of my language which meant much to me as I loved to write and was an avid reader. Perhaps underlying my fear of emigrating was the memory of the earlier separations of my childhood: from our home and, of course, from my father. These separations left painful memories deeply embedded in my subconscious. Every subsequent change in my life, which entailed leaving people and places I was attached to, caused me a tremendous sense of panic and fear. I would have done anything to avoid facing such anxiety.

But in the spring of 1950 such a situation was presenting itself again. I felt heartbroken. I did not want to leave behind all that had sustained me so richly after the dark years of the war. Yet there was also a part of me which felt some excitement at the prospect of a possible adventure, at escaping from the restrictions of the communist regime, and at seeing something of another part of the world. Perhaps most of all, part of me wished to leave a country where I had had to lie about my Jewish identity for so long and still felt impelled to do so. I loved Poland. It was the country of my birth. Its language, landscape, music and character were an inextricable part of me, yet at the same time I felt an outsider to a large degree because of the insidious depth and intensity of anti-Semitism there.

Sadly, this prejudice was illustrated by an incident I experienced not long before we left Poland for Israel. I was on a train, returning to Katowice from a nearby place I had been visiting. In the compartment where I was sitting, some fellow travellers were engaged in conversation on a subject I don't recollect, but which gradually developed into an extremely negative anti-Semitic conversation. I sat listening to this as my inner anger intensified. I felt grateful that Mother and I would never again witness this Polish hatred of Jews, not withstanding our deep gratitude to the wonderful Poles who had helped us to survive. When the train arrived at my destination, on leaving the compartment I turned to my fellow travellers and said 'I have been listening to all you spoke of with great interest as I happen to be a Jew!' They sat there in embarrassed silence.

At that time, I was a young girl full of dreams and hopes, anticipating a wonderful future, yet having to confront a conflict caused by this complex situation. I knew that there was no question of our staying in Poland, particularly now, after the creation of a Jewish state. We had been beaten enough into realising how unwanted we were in Poland. That fact I was deeply aware of, yet at the same time my heart sank in fear of going somewhere unknown with the expectation of facing hardship. So often in life I have found that the things we anticipate never turn out to be quite what we either feared or hoped for. In the case of that crucial change in our lives in 1950 it also proved to be so. It is true that many difficulties lay ahead of us as immigrants to a two-year-old newly created state, but so many new possibilities arose with this situation which we could not have foreseen.

In leaving the communist regime which took control of Poland after liberating it from Nazi cruelty and virtual slavery, we were leaving behind a country which was not truly free. Poland had become a subservient satellite state within Stalin's Soviet empire where personal freedom was vastly restricted. Anyone who did not completely toe the line of the official regime's political persuasion and propaganda, could find themselves in serious difficulties. To express words of criticism of anything stemming from Poland's 'liberators' – the Soviet Union and its great leader Stalin, along with his entire political entourage – could become a ticket to exile in Siberia. This was a horrifying prospect of internment in the most alien and harsh conditions. We had to be constantly on our guard against openly saying anything that could be interpreted as anti-Soviet or anti-communist. Such remarks spelled danger. So, although we no longer needed to hide our religious, ethnic identity for fear of being put to death, we were still not truly free.

My mother made all the preparations for getting a permit to leave Poland. I kept silent about it until the last days before our journey out of the country when I told my piano teacher, who had such high hopes for me as a pianist in Poland. Even at that point Mother decided that it would not be right for us to divulge the whole truth about ourselves and we only mentioned that we were leaving Poland to go to Paris, where Mother's brother, Uncle Max, had gone to live a while before. It would have been too embarrassing, and almost cruel, to tell people who were close to us and liked us sincerely, but who also quite casually showed their typical dislike of and prejudice against the Jews, that we were in fact Jewish and were now leaving to become citizens of our own new Jewish state.

In May 1950, having given up our modest home, renounced our Polish citizenship and taking with us only those personal belongings which we could pack, we set off on our journey to the Promised Land. To our knowledge, at that time, the promise was one of life in a hot climate, frugal conditions, a very fragile and tentative state of peace, a language with no European roots, and therefore quite strange to our ears and eyes (Hebrew also looks strange) – in short, a promise of struggle. We had no money, no home to go to, no furniture and no piano. There was, however, one thing which proved to be of value in my musical pursuits in Israel. This was my letter of introduction to Frank Pelleg, the man responsible for music at the Ministry of Education and Culture in Jerusalem.

When I think of the decision my brave mother took at that point, I cannot fail to admire her for her courage, obvious intelligence and an intuition for the right direction to take in our lives. I was, of course, lamenting in my heart the fact that I was leaving my musical life and education behind, which I was told might mean the end of all my dreams of becoming a pianist. But my mother, then in her mid-life, took a far greater risk. Her work depended on a knowledge of the language. She was leaving her job as an office worker in a government ministry. She could not at that time have had any hope of being able to find some parallel occupation in Israel without a knowledge of Hebrew – a very difficult language which has absolutely nothing in common with either Polish or German, both of which she spoke fluently. I wonder what trepidation accompanied her on her way to the new land? She did not let me see any of her apprehensions and doubts, though I am certain she must have had many. An added difficulty for Mother must have been the fact that we were going without my sister and her husband. We planned that, at some point we would try to join them in Australia, to where they were emigrating, though there was no certainty about that. (Thanks to a relative whom my brother-in-law discovered in Australia, he and Jasia were able to move there together.) Surprisingly they were given a permit to leave for Australia at about the same time as we were allowed to join the emigration to Israel. Our small family discussed various probabilities of a reunion once we were out of the communist country with all its restrictions on personal freedom.

Julian and Jasia – or Janette as she was later called – left for Paris en route to Melbourne. Mother, her younger sister Marysia who lived with us in Katowice, and I travelled to Israel via Italy. We encountered no luxury on our train journey to Venice, nor on the ship which took us from there to Haifa, though all the experiences had an air of excitement for me in spite of the uncertainty of what was to come.

The moment of arriving in the port of Haifa, and stepping out on to the soil of a country which was a true home for the Jews, was a most moving one. It was like a dream for so many of us who were filled with still-fresh memories of the Holocaust. Many people were crying; some literally knelt down to kiss the ground. There were very emotional scenes amongst people leaving the ship; some were meeting relatives, while most were being received by Israeli officials who were to place us in temporary transit camps.

We were taken to a vast immigrants' transit camp which consisted of many large tents equipped with small metal-framed beds. Each person was given a blanket and each family some primitive cooking equipment to prepare basic meals; this was usually just a primus stove. We and our modest belongings were liberally sprinkled with DDT disinfectant powder to prevent an outbreak of infectious diseases. The place was a veritable Tower of Babel. All of us were Jewish people, but each group from a different geographic region and speaking a different language, our cultural conditions and social customs as diverse as the lands we came from.

The people from Eastern Europe could communicate with the help of some German or Yiddish. People from Slavic countries put together fragments of their respective Slavic languages and tried to converse in this often-confusing way. Here we were in our own homeland and yet, in so many ways, because of the inherited cultures of our native lands, we were like strangers to this new country and to each other. That was the first difficulty one experienced, not to mention the harsh conditions of living in a camp, without even having one's own private living space. There was, of course, a common language – Hebrew – but that was known only to those born in the land, or those who had come to live there before Israel became an independent state. We were yet to learn that language in order to be integrated into the society and not to remain part-foreigners. Meanwhile people were gradually leaving the Haifa camp (it was called Sha'ar Ha'aliya – the 'Gate of Ascent' or 'Gate to Immigration') to other parts of the country where they were hoping to settle.

The three of us, Mother, Aunt Marysia and I, chose to go to Jerusalem where we hoped to find some opportunities for me to study, although we had no money to buy a home and certainly no hope of having our own piano. In Jerusalem, we were installed in a large immigrants' camp which had been set up in disused army barracks previously belonging to the British Army. Here too we shared a large space with several other families, this time in an old barracks building rather than a tent. Jerusalem is situated within a beautiful landscape of high hills. The evenings often had a cool breeze which brought welcome relief from the heat of the day's sun. Because of the better climate, Jerusalem was an attractive place for people seeking to spend a few days away from the oppressive heat in other parts of the country.

Soon after we came to the Jerusalem camp my mother found manual work in a nearby private holiday guest house. We needed money and had to look for the means not only to provide for our daily needs but also to get out of the depressing life of the camp. Conditions in this camp, in which each family had only a few beds and a primitive cooker, and lived in public, as it were, within the large tin-roofed barracks building, were truly awful. Israel, at that time, had very little to offer the large influx of newcomers from many countries in Europe and the Middle East. We discovered that Yiddish did not help in trying to communicate with one's brethren who had been driven out in hundreds and thousands from countries like Morocco, Algiers, Tunisia and Yemen. They spoke Arabic and some French. Jews who for generations had spoken Arabic were culturally quite alien to European Jews. Their only common ground was the Old Testament, and religious ceremonies and traditions, as well as – now – their own homeland where they would no longer be persecuted. But there was often a high price to be paid for this freedom which had not been ours for some two thousand years. The price of giving one's life in the struggle for it – the highest price a human can pay. We also had to face various hardships arising from the difficulties of bringing large numbers of people, of so many diverse backgrounds, into an undeveloped country. There were countless difficulties: shortage of meat, fish and many other foods – even fruit was limited – although there was plenty of citrus fruit, but only in season. Otherwise we went short of so many food products which are now to be found in Israel in abundance. Many items were rationed.

The number of homes being built, as rapidly as possible, was quite insufficient to accommodate the thousands of new immigrants. The cost of apartments was very high and beyond the reach of many of the almost penniless newcomers. To afford some commodities, such as a fridge, gas cooker or washing machine, one had to be very well off. These items, though quite indispensable for the climate and daily necessities in a home were, in Israel's conditions at the time, considered the height of luxury. We were able to acquire simple ice-boxes in which some of our food could be protected from rotting in the heat of the middle-eastern climate. There were two main types of street vendors travelling on donkey-drawn carts, who announced their presence from quite some distance by ringing a loud hand-bell. One of these was a man who delivered kerosene for our heaters or cookers, while the other sold large blocks of ice for the primitive ice-coolers in which food was kept.

CHAPTER 17

Henrietta Michaelson and the Jerusalem Music Academy

The idea of trying to pursue a young girl's desire to be a pianist would have seemed an unrealistic, impossible aim in our general situation, which was fraught with the problems of daily existence, as well as those of security caused by continual shooting incidents across the borders of what was a very small – narrow and long – country. Perhaps reality can change against all apparent odds if a wish and desire for something is so strong that it has to find its fulfilment.

A strange set of coincidences began to lead me, in unexpected ways, towards being able to resume my development as a musician. We had no piano – Uncle Max, to whom we already owed so much for helping us during the war, again extended his helping hand to my mother. Although he was not too affluent as an émigré in Paris he was obviously better off than we were at the time, and therefore sent us some money to help with our most immediate needs, including, eventually, enabling us to buy a frugal one-room home to live in. We felt very fortunate and were grateful for his kindness. However, my mother needed to earn a regular income and had therefore to undertake whatever work she could find. She was first offered simple domestic work in a private guest house in the Jerusalem hills. The place often hosted quite sophisticated members of Israel's intellectual and artistic community. Among the guests were artists who had lived in the country before the state of Israel was established, having arrived there just before or during the war as refugees from Nazism. One such person was a very fine singing teacher, Frau Boroschek, originally from Berlin, who came to Palestine in the thirties to escape from Hitler's Germany. She happened to be a guest at the pension when my mother began working there. Mother lost no time in talking to the owner of the house, a very remarkable Russian-born woman, Mrs Kornberg, about the wonderfully gifted daughter she had. Mrs Kornberg must have been treated to quite some eulogies about my mother's wonderful teenage child, whose talent had been so greatly praised and acknowledged in Poland.

One can well imagine Mrs Kornberg's thoughts and reservations. Isn't every Jewish mother's daughter extraordinarily beautiful, most gifted and unique! Knowing my mother's tenacity whenever she set her mind to achieving something, I expect she gently persisted with her story until she encountered a positive response. Mrs Kornberg suggested that Mother bring me with her one day to meet the well-known singing teacher, Frau Boroschek from Berlin, who knew much of what was happening in music circles and music education in Israel. After meeting me, she said I ought to be introduced to a very distinguished person who had recently arrived from New York to settle in Jerusalem. This was Henrietta Michaelson, a retired piano teacher from the Juilliard School in New York where she had taught for 35 years. Having retired she decided to spend her remaining years in Israel where she hoped to make a contribution in her own field of expertise. I was told that she would listen to my playing and if she thought me really talented, then we should try to find some means of continuing my studies. Who knows? She herself might even offer to help towards that end.

A few days later I was taken to meet Miss Michaelson. She was a tall, impressive-looking woman in her mid-sixties with a very commanding presence. Asked if I spoke English I said 'Yes', counting on my five years of English classes at school to prove of practical use now. However, after her first few words I realised my real ignorance of the English language that I was supposed to have learned at school in Poland. I therefore said: '*Bitte sprechen sie Deutsch*' ('Please speak German'), as I hoped she could. Although I had not had German tuition at school (unlike my five years of English!) I had heard much German spoken on my mother's side of the family whenever something was discussed which the children were not supposed to know about. In fact, by the time the war came, my mother was surprised to discover that I could understand and even speak German. And I now found that Henrietta Michaelson could also speak German, so this was the language in which we were able to communicate, at first. Later I learned that, as a young woman, Henrietta had spent some time studying in Vienna where she acquired her knowledge of German. My audition for her was an unqualified success. Immediately after hearing me play she began to discuss with me what I should prepare for my lesson with her the following week. She had taken me on as her pupil in that instant. I was absolutely thrilled. It all seemed better than I could have hoped for. However, although I was pleased at the prospect of returning to my piano studies, particularly with this distinguished teacher, I worriedly told her that I had no piano to practise on in preparation for my lessons. Henrietta did not seem to consider this a serious obstacle at the time. She looked at me and asked if I had seriously studied music theory in Poland, especially the theory of Western music harmony. 'Yes, I did' was my reply. In that case, until a place with a piano for me to practise on could be found, she said I could learn new works of music and memorise them from the score without the use of the instrument. I must say no one had ever suggested this to me in my previous studies. As far as I knew, one always needed an instrument on which to learn a piece of music. This new way of working on music developed for me, in successive years, a most valuable technique with practical value when travelling and in other situations in which no piano is available. A study of music away from the instrument also gave me a clearer understanding of structural details of the composition.

Henrietta Michaelson, this remarkable person, had acknowledged that I was talented and she not only wanted me to become her pupil but took it upon herself to try to help me and my mother in every way she could. Within days of our meeting she had dispatched letters to some of her wealthy friends in New York whom she knew were very keen on supporting Israel. She wrote to them about the gifted young girl who had recently arrived from Poland, was living in conditions of considerable poverty and needed anything that could be offered to her. Soon parcels began to arrive at her home filled with all kinds of goods – especially clothes. I began to receive so many new things to wear that we did not need to spend money (which, in any case, we were very short of) on any garments.

By an extraordinary coincidence, only a short while after my meeting with Myckie (which is what Henrietta's friends and students always called her), someone from the same apartment building in which she lived in Jerusalem offered us a very small room to live in. This meant we could leave the immigrants' camp, which would at least afford us – that is my mother, Aunt Marysia and me – a degree of privacy that was otherwise completely impossible in the Talpioth camp, where 12 families shared an open existence in each of the large old army barrack buildings.

The place we moved to was a tiny, narrow room with one window overlooking a courtyard. There was just enough space in it for the three beds we had been given at the camp, as well as a little table on which our faithful little primus cooker was placed. Here Mother prepared our meals. We had to sit on one of the beds to eat, as there was no room for any chairs in our little 'home'. We were given a key to the apartment of our benefactor, Mrs Parnas, to whom the little room belonged. In her apartment, we had access to a bathroom. All this, though less than basic, constituted a great improvement in our living conditions. What was more, the very kind Mrs Parnas invited me to make use of her piano. I was able to go in each day to practise for one or two hours. The Parnas family lived on the ground floor in the same building as Myckie, who occupied an apartment on the top floor.

After some time, Uncle Max, in his great generosity, sent my mother the money to buy a small, independent dwelling consisting of just one room in a disused, dilapidated house on the border of divided Jerusalem, between the (Arab) Jordanian and Israeli sectors. There was constant danger of being hit by a bullet, as snipers in the Arab part of Jerusalem could see us coming and going. We often had to almost crawl to avoid being noticed by the snipers. However, it was the first place Mother and I could call home. (Aunt Marysia had, by then, moved to Tel Aviv where she married and settled down.)

Uncle Max also did something of tremendous significance for me. He sent a piano to us from Paris. This was the most loving act towards me and, of course, a source of great joy to my mother, who so wished for me to continue my musical development.

All these changes in our life occurred within a short time of my becoming Henrietta Michaelson's pupil. Other important things happened for me too. Myckie arranged for me to become a scholarship student at the Music Academy of Jerusalem. This meant that the Academy, which was run as a kind of co-operative of some of the best musicians in the country, allowed me to participate in all classes and lectures without a fee. In other words, I had a full scholarship throughout my studies. But it also meant that Henrietta Michaelson was not paid for teaching me. Amongst my teachers at the Jerusalem Academy were some of the finest musicians in Jerusalem at the time – including Joseph Tal the composer and pianist, Paul Ben-Haim, one of the best known of Israel's composers, Chaim Alexander and Abba Erlich. Most of these musicians were refugees from Hitler's Europe. Several had been amongst the elite of the music community in pre-war Germany, as well as in other countries. Those of us who became their students in the early fifties had the good fortune of being steeped, through them, in the best of European musical traditions. The conditions we worked in were very basic, to say the least. There were hardly any really good instruments in the small, though picturesque-looking, old building which housed the Academy in the very centre of Jerusalem. The piano used for students' concerts was one which Henrietta Michaelson had donated on her arrival from the States. However, there were some extremely gifted and clever young students amongst my colleagues. A number of them came into prominence in Israel's music community as well as subsequently establishing international reputations. Amongst them were the piano duo Bracha Eden and Alexander Tamir, Dalia Atlas, the first Israeli woman conductor and the wonderful soprano Netania Davrath. I heard Netania's moving singing in many concerts in Israel and later, in London, when she was the soloist in Mahler's fourth symphony at The Royal Festival Hall. After the performance a critic in *The Times* wrote: 'This is a voice one dreams of but seldom hears.'

It was during my first year of being Henrietta Michaelson's student at the Music Academy that Mother suggested I should contact Frank Pelleg, for whom I had the letter of introduction from the Israeli Consulate in Warsaw. We found his office in Jerusalem and I went with the letter (without knowing its contents) to meet him.

My first meeting with Frank Pelleg was somewhat amusing. He spoke Czech to me and I answered in Polish. Somehow this mode of communication was apparently sufficient for him to gather whatever it was he wanted to know about me. My main request at that time was for some help in finding a piano on which to practise. To this end, he gave me a letter written in Hebrew (which, of course, I could not read or understand) to one of the main producers in the music department of Kol Israel – the Israel Broadcasting Service ('Voice of Israel'). I was received at the studio and told I could come to practise each morning for some time. However, what I did not know until some months later, was that in the letter Frank Pelleg suggested to the producer that he listen to my playing, because I might be very gifted. Indeed, to my utter surprise and amazement, a few days after I began practising at the studio the producer, Arieh Sachs – himself an accomplished musician – asked me to give a 15-minute piano recital for Kol Israel. This immediately led to further radio engagements. It was through these early radio recitals that my performing career in Israel began, while I was still a student. Henrietta Michaelson was delighted with these initial successes, and she worked very devotedly in preparing me for each performance. She always voiced her great hopes for my future as a pianist and gave me much encouragement. Two years later, at a concert given by students of the Music Academy, I met Frank Pelleg and asked him why he had recommended me to the radio producer without having heard me play. His reply sounded almost facetious but I knew he really meant it. He said 'I could tell from the expression in your eyes that you had talent.'

CHAPTER 18

The Mozart Competition and Public Concerts

One day, in the second year of my studies with Henrietta, I arrived at her house for a piano lesson and was greeted by her showing me an advertisement in the paper. It announced a National Competition for young performers playing music by Mozart. Henrietta looked at me and said: 'This is a Mozart competition for pianists and violinists and you will take part and certainly win the first prize'. I was taken aback. It was almost as if she regarded the outcome to be a foregone conclusion. In my great respect and admiration for Myckie, whom I considered to be such an outstanding teacher, and in my innocent, youthful trust in her judgement, I thought that it most probably had to be as she said. I applied to take part in the competition. A good number of other young pianists and violinists also took part. Amongst the judges were various fine musicians and in the finals the great Chilean pianist Claudio Arrau presided over the jury. I did win first prize. Myckie was right. Was it her certainty that I would win that added extra confidence to my playing? I wonder. There is no doubt that her confidence in my ability encouraged me enormously and spurred me on to do the best I could.

I prepared for the competition while living with my mother and aunt in our little room in the courtyard, without a piano of my own. However, I was able to make use of someone else's piano for two hours every morning, and practise for a short time each day at the apartment of Mr and Mrs Parnas, who never showed the slightest sign that they were disturbed by it; they were always most welcoming and generous. I also spent some of the time sitting in a little public garden in the centre of Jerusalem, studying the music quietly from the score and going over details of it in my mind. This consisted of a Mozart sonata and piano concerto as well as a short work by an Israeli composer. Over the years this approach led to my developing a considerable ability to learn music not at the piano, but by studying a score – working on absorbing its contents mentally and committing it to memory in its entirety – before actually trying to play it. Eventually this method also entered the core of my teaching.

What was particularly exciting about winning the Mozart competition was that the first prize was a free flight from Tel Aviv to Amsterdam, where one of the wealthiest Dutch families received me as their guest for a week, while I attended the wonderful concerts and other performances at the – for me – fascinating Holland Festival. All this was an incredibly exciting event in the life of a youngster not so long out of the horrors of a Polish ghetto, and living and studying in conditions of considerable poverty.

In fact, despite all the gloomy predictions of no future for me as a musician once I left Poland, I was, through a succession of coincidences, not only continuing my studies again but being taught by the most remarkable teacher I had yet encountered. Above all I was taking my first steps towards becoming a professional pianist. How unpredictable life's paths can be.

However, the frugal conditions of our daily life at the time were not the only difficulties in the early years of my life in Israel. One thing accompanied me constantly throughout the varying circumstances of my life and that was the haunted nature of my unconscious inner life. Dreams of danger, persecution, violence and fear came to me every night and subtly hidden anxieties were present in my days too. I continued to have the nightmares which in Poland were based on scenes from the Nazi occupation. Interestingly enough the identity of the threatening figures began to change gradually, so that instead of being chased by the SS who were trying to kill me, I began to be threatened by Arab figures. It is quite fascinating to think that the dreams and reality were not so vastly different. There we were, Jews from various European countries, most of whom had survived the Holocaust in near miraculous ways, gathered now in a country that was to be, finally, after so many generations, our own home. Israel was to be a symbol of freedom and security for us. Yet it existed under the constant strain of threats and attacks aimed at us from across all our borders. In Israel we could regain our sense of human dignity; we could feel, express fully and enjoy our Jewish identity; and we could relish the sense of being independent in our own homeland, rather than being a guilt-ridden persecuted minority in another country. But one thing we did not experience – the one thing that we war survivors particularly longed for – was a sense of peace and security. All able-bodied men and women from the age of 18 were conscripted into the army and were trained to help defend the country, which was constantly attacked in small- or larger-scale incidents.

In these situations, I saw the difference between my own reactions to danger from attack and those of my contemporaries who had been born and brought up in the country. I experienced great insecurity, anxiety and downright fear – all feelings which were deeply entrenched in me since the war years in Poland. On the other hand, the Sabras (as the Israeli-born were called) remained calm and collected, and went about their business without signs of fear or panic. Even though, without doubt, they must have occasionally felt fear, they always gave an impression of being in command of the situation, whereas I more often than not reacted as if I were a victim.

For me, life in Israel in those days was full of contrasting experiences. On the one hand there was the excitement of new developments in my musical life with the help of Henrietta Michaelson's remarkable teaching, my first professional engagements in recitals on radio and with an orchestra; on the other hand, there were also many hardships in our day-to-day life. Our accommodation was basic, to say the least. We had little money, and had it not been for the help we received from several people we would have had hardly enough for food or clothing.

As I have mentioned before, Uncle Max knew of the great difficulties we experienced in Israel and, in spite of not being too well-off himself, sent us a little money from time to time. This was of great help to us, especially when Mother gave up her work at the Kornberg guest house after we moved away from the immigrants' camp. She took an intensive six-month course in Hebrew, in the hope that she would be able to return to office work once she had mastered the language, at least to some degree. The physical work was not only a strain on her energy, but also frustrating and limiting in the extreme for someone of her intelligence and spirit. The course was gruelling, but Mother plunged into it so that she could learn at least the basics of the language of Israel. My mother was a woman of great strength of character and tenacity, and had ability to take the trouble to achieve what she felt was necessary, even if it required enormous effort on her part. Learning the Hebrew language was, at that stage of her life, no mean venture in the best of circumstances. Trying to do it, however, while living in our very frugal and uncomfortable conditions was a truly admirable undertaking. She spent days at her school and in the evenings, by the light of a kerosene lamp (there was no electricity in our little room), she did her homework.

The process of absorbing a new language was very much easier for me. Presumably my youth and a good ear, not only for music but also for languages, gave me a vast advantage over Mother. Within a few months of my attending lectures and classes at the Music Academy (where, of course, no one wanted to teach anything but music-related subjects), I began to understand increasingly more Hebrew and by degrees started to speak it. My early attempts at conversing with Israeli colleagues in Hebrew were naturally tentative and I leant heavily on support from English, German and even Latin or occasional Yiddish expressions when all else failed. However, I found myself speaking Hebrew ever more fluently during my first year as a student at the Academy.

For me, those early times in Israel were filled with much emotional magic, which came from my encounters with music. With Henrietta's guidance and encouragement, I was making great strides in my development as a pianist. Myckie thought that I had a definite future as a performer. Although I encountered many setbacks along the way, due to both external circumstances and the legacy of emotional difficulties from my wartime childhood, her predictions about my future were proved right. I did go on working as a musician and continued to learn and to search for ways of improving, and broadening my knowledge of and ability in performing music.

This led me to something that added an unexpected, rich and enlightening new dimension to my life in general, and to my work as a pianist in particular. Through Henrietta, I became acquainted with the existence of a teaching called the Alexander Technique. Henrietta had met and had lessons from F.M. Alexander, the originator of the Technique. On coming to live in Israel she had brought with her books by F.M. Alexander about his work, and she told me much about his remarkable teaching. Hardly a piano lesson went by in which Myckie would not try to elucidate something about her approach to playing in the light of what she had learned from Alexander. I heard about how Alexander had developed the Technique to improve a person's overall co-ordination. However, Myckie repeatedly told all of her students that to learn this Technique we had to be guided by an experienced and specially trained teacher, and she was not qualified to give us such guidance.

It was not until 1960 that an unexpected opportunity to learn the Alexander Technique presented itself; with it came many other developments in my personal and professional life. Before that, however, I continued to study and perform in Israel, always under Henrietta Michaelson's tutelage. I gave regular radio recitals, performed concertos with the Radio Symphony Orchestra, gave recitals in kibbutzim* (communal agricultural settlements) and went on to gain my degree in teaching and performing from the Rubin Academy of Music in Jerusalem.

Shortly after my graduation from the Academy I was invited to join three other young musicians to form a quartet. There were two flautists, a married couple called Sharona and Chanoch Tel-Oren, who had come from the United States to settle in Israel, and a cellist, Paul Blassberger, originally from Hungary. The couple, though only in their twenties, were well known as first and second flautists in Jerusalem's Radio Symphony Orchestra. We began to play together, invited several Israeli composers to write works for our unusual ensemble and began to appear in many chamber music concerts throughout Israel under the name Dalet Klei Shir (which literally translates as 'Four Instruments of Song').

Playing in the quartet provided wonderful experience of making music with others and also of going on tours to various kibbutzim all over the country (which all four of

* Kibbutzim – plural of kibbutz

us enjoyed enormously). This was my first experience of going on short concert tours and I learnt much from it as a performer. The conditions for a pianist performing in the kibbutzim in the fifties were not at all easy. There were no good pianos to play on: mostly they were absolutely worn out old instruments of a kind that later in my professional life I would never agree to perform on. Yet in those days I loved going on tour with the quartet, meeting many different people and feeding off a range of experiences and encounters. Our programmes included music for the whole ensemble from the eighteenth and twentieth centuries as well as solo piano works, mainly from the nineteenth-century repertoire. The concerts were very popular amongst the kibbutzim and were very well received in chamber music series in Tel Aviv and Jerusalem.

Sometimes we found ourselves in awkward and funny situations – like, for example, arriving to give a concert at a very young kibbutz where all the members were under 30 (they had just celebrated the arrival of the first baby on their kibbutz), only to be told that their piano had no pedals. We (particularly me) looked in astonishment at a grand piano standing in the corner of the communal dining room with only an empty space where the pedals should be. After some detective work on my part we discovered that some pieces of the old piano pedals were to be found in the work shed. Within half an hour, with the help of the kibbutz carpenter and a number of other young men, a newly constructed pro-visional pedal was attached to the piano. An hour later our concert started, and as soon as I played the first phrase and used the pedal the whole audience gave a loud cheer. The pedal consisted of two small pieces of board attached by rods to the dampers of the piano and it worked like a charm.

The atmosphere at these kibbutz concerts was quite informal – any member of the kibbutz was free to come in to listen, and if he or she did not like what they heard they simply walked out. In the early days of kibbutz concerts, we used to joke that we might start with a large audience and end up playing only to the dedicated few after the rest had gradually left, too bored to listen to classical music at the end of a day's hard work in the field, tending chickens, or looking after children. However, this never happened to us. Quite the reverse often occurred, as more and more people would put their heads round the communal dining room 'concert hall' door, listen to a bit, then come in and stay for the rest of the evening. We were very gratified at feeling the genuine pleasure these people derived from listening to our music. They were a very special audience indeed.

These concerts gave me an opportunity to find out increasingly more about the vicissitudes of performing in public, as well as the excitement of the shared musical experience. Each round of concert giving would have me raring to go on working towards a higher level of playing, adding to the repertoire, and constantly aiming for the ideal performances which are somehow always just out of reach. Now, many years later, I think that the moment I cease striving for ever better performances of music is the moment I should stop giving concerts.

CHAPTER 19

Marriage to Gabriel Ben-Or

Some two years after our arrival in Israel there was a crucial development in our lives, which changed the course of my professional future. My mother was unexpectedly asked to go to Melbourne to be with my sister, who had, by now, anglicised her name Jasia to Janette. The war experiences had finally taken their toll and Janette who, together with her husband, had emigrated to Australia two years earlier, became very seriously ill. Her doctors, as well as my brother-in-law, thought that it would be beneficial for her to have Mother near her. Our brave mother, who by then had struggled out of her Hebrew illiteracy through hard study, had not long before found employment at one of the main offices of the Israel Ministry of Health. When the news of my sister's illness came, Mother was quite devastated and knew that she had to go to Australia to be near her.

Around that time, I met a young Israeli architect and within a short period decided to marry him. Being very young I took the idea of marriage to be a simple and easy undertaking – not realising what it might really mean. My mother was very unhappy about my decision, and thought that I was far too young for marriage and that my prospective husband was not really suitable for me. This could have been simply a mother's natural reaction to her daughter's early marriage. However, in this case, Mother's misgivings later proved to be well-founded. But in 1952 I decided to get married and my mother went to Melbourne for what was supposed to be a temporary stay. In the event Australia became her permanent home to the end of her life.

For me the marriage became an often tough learning ground in the first serious steps along the path to growing up. My husband, Gabriel (known as Gabi), proved to be a young man of completely different cultural and emotional make-up to my own. These vast differences soon became evident in our relationship. He was a tough young Israeli, born in Jerusalem 22 years before the creation of the state of Israel. He was of mixed parentage, in that his mother came from an old Sephardic family in Jerusalem and his father had come to Palestine from Poland some years before World War II.

Gabi was the sort of middle-eastern man whose ideas about relationships between men and women were quite stereotyped and they ruled his emotional attitudes with great rigidity. In his mind men and women each had a clearly defined role to play in marriage, along with specific tasks to carry out. For Gabi, fidelity in sexual relations was of absolute and paramount importance, and one false step in this regard would mean the end of the marriage. He expected strict adherence to this rule not only of me but also of himself. He was unyielding and inflexible in many matters in life, both large and small. According to his idea of our respective roles, I was to look after everything relating to housekeeping, which did also allow for getting help with some of the physical work. On one occasion, when I asked Gabi to help me clear up after a meal, he looked angry and said stubbornly, 'I don't want to – that is your job'. This was his characteristic response in many similar circumstances.

However there was, of course, another and very attractive side to him. He was extremely sensitive to good music, and had a keen eye for beauty, both in nature and in art. His creative gifts were very apparent – not only in architecture, his profession – but also in painting, pottery and the making of various objects for the house.

We were married during the time I was studying at the Music Academy. Having been used to my mother looking after all the practical daily necessities at home, so that I could devote most of my time to my studies and to piano playing, marriage came as something of a shock. My relationship with Gabi became a subtle battleground for a position of authority or superiority; a battle in which each one of us felt unfairly treated by the other. I still believe that our immaturity did not afford us the opportunity to negotiate an easier exchange of duties between us. But, above all, it was the inflexibility of Gabi's preconceived ideas of what a wife's duties in marriage were (which would be quite unacceptable to most modern couples) that sowed the seeds of discontent between us. The matter was further complicated for me by an aspect of my personality that gradually emerged during the years of my marriage to Gabi: my deep insecurity and sense of helplessness. This made me dependent on him and quite terrified of a possible separation. The almost pathological fear of losing my new home and of saying goodbye to someone with whom I was sharing my life (unsatisfactory though it happened to be) was so great that it rendered me unable to do anything about my situation. I found the difficulties in my marriage often hard to put up with, but even the thought of ending it left me paralysed with fear.

Separation and the loss of a home were experiences that I was desperate to avoid. They sparked memories of past experiences so fraught with pain that I could not come anywhere near to allowing a repetition of them. Our relationship continued with many moments of tension and dissatisfaction. Somewhere deep inside me I knew that it would not last, but I felt unable to do anything about it. There was a great difference in our mentalities, as well as in our emotional make-up and, although we were both Jewish, we had been brought up in two different cultures and that set us apart in many respects.

Above all I think that I was still suffering psychologically from the Holocaust, feeling very insecure and frightened. Gabi could not quite understand this, as he himself was of that strong and brave breed of young Palestinian Jews who became the original creators and defenders of the state of Israel. The kind of fears that became so deeply ingrained in my psyche were incomprehensible to him and, on the whole, he was insensitive to them. I continued to have very powerful nightmares. The pattern of a terrifying dream occurring almost every night, so that I would awake screaming or crying, continued in just the same way as before my marriage. Although Gabi realised that my past was not conventional or easy, he could not relate to its reality, and so become a bit more sympathetic and flexible in our relationship. He did his best, as far as he could – so did I, as far as I could – but we did not really form a relationship that had a chance of developing and deepening. We both suffered: I from his inflexibility and he from my not behaving according to his ideal. We remained married for over seven years, a long time for two young people. During those years, however, I gradually developed as a pianist, completed my formal musical studies and was invited to teach at the Jerusalem Academy of Music. I took part in concerts, gave regular broadcasts and, of course, travelled frequently with the quartet to perform in many kibbutzim and chamber music centres. Gabi, meanwhile, worked in town planning at the Ministry of the Interior.

Throughout those years I continued to study with Henrietta Michaelson and was guided by her in many respects, not only musically. She was a woman of great charisma and strength – many young people respected and admired her immensely. Her influence on those who studied with her was far-reaching and, in some cases, changed the direction of their lives. She certainly had a significant effect on my own development, particularly as I was at a young and impressionable age when she first took me on as her pupil.

Life in Jerusalem during my student days was very intense. The Israeli sector of the city (west Jerusalem) was not large and was divided from east Jerusalem, which was the Jordanian sector. There were areas near the border between the two sectors which remained danger zones: snipers from the Arab part of the city would often aim at people on the Israeli side. We learned which areas to stay away from in order to avoid being on the receiving end of a sniper's bullet.

There were always economic difficulties and, although people working on the land gradually began to produce more fruit, vegetables and other foods, there were shortages of various goods and commodities; cars in particular were considered an extreme luxury. However, there was always much artistic activity, especially in music. It was a time when a number of musicians – such as the young Daniel Barenboim and Alice Herz-Sommer – came to prominence in Israel and later established wide-ranging international careers. (Alice Herz-Sommer was an emigré from Prague; years later we became good friends after she came to live in London for the last two decades of her life.)

I began to feel somewhat restricted in what was, after all a rather small arena for musical pursuits, particularly considering the number of musicians in the country. After playing with the Dalet Klei Shir quartet for several years, and gaining much experience in performing chamber music as well as solo, I decided that the time had come for me to develop my playing further and I therefore gave up appearing with the quartet. We were all sad to part company as we had grown close and had many interesting and happy experiences as an ensemble. We had become good friends and naturally had much in common. Travelling around the country, we had shared many amusing moments and developed our own particular brand of humour around the types of people we encountered. On these journeys, we learnt about the distinct differences of character between a kibbutz whose members had an eastern European background and one with members of Anglo-Saxon origin. We could predict their reactions to our programme, our playing and our appearance. We would often burst into cascades of laughter in the dressing room at some subtle remark that one of us had made about our audience. We laughed at ourselves, particularly at our very easy-going cellist and his amusing, broad Hungarian accent. We had much joy and fun in our preparation for concerts and in playing at so many different venues. Yet, I did come to the point where I felt it necessary for me to leave the quartet and change my professional direction.

Giving up my commitment to the quartet meant that I could devote more time to working on music for solo piano. I also needed a change from the routine of playing the rather limited repertoire suitable for our unusual combination of instruments. There was so much music for piano by great composers which I longed to learn to play, rather than repeatedly practising and performing the same works for our concerts, season after season. My relationship with Gabi was deteriorating. Henrietta, as well as various close friends, began advising me to get a divorce. The idea frightened me. The prospect of being quite alone and without sufficient money of my own deterred me from leaving Gabi. But, I think the real reasons for my reluctance to end my marriage were my deep-rooted fear of separation and my anxiety about loneliness.

CHAPTER 20

Death of Henrietta and Divorce from Gabi

In 1959 an event occurred which was a great emotional upheaval for me and for a number of other young people, as well as for various friends: Henrietta Michaelson suffered a stroke and died shortly afterwards. She was 75 and had spent the last ten years of her life living and teaching in Israel. Her death was a shock to many, because she played a vital role in music education in Israel and was a significant figure in the artistic life of Jerusalem. That city, in which she chose to live out her last decade, was at the time also home to many fine intellectuals, musicians and artists who, in spite of the restricted size of the divided city, gave it a special atmosphere of intense intellectual and spiritual presence. Henrietta Michaelson was very much a part of that core of Jerusalem's artistic and sophisticated intellectual milieu. To me her death signified the end of my formative years as a pianist. It was also a deeply felt personal loss. Myckie was not only my teacher but also my friend and mentor, whose influence on my development was of great significance. Over the years, I could see how much I had gained from her teaching and her friendship. Admittedly later, as I began to pave my own way as a musician, I came to see many things in my own different way; however, her teaching had sown the seeds for such later development. The most important of these was my interest in the Alexander Technique, which eventually led to the opening of an important new chapter in my life.

Henrietta Michaelson's death was also a very important cathartic experience for me. She was the first close person in my life who died a natural death, whom I was able to mourn and whose burial I witnessed. There was a sense of completion of a life, rather than a violent cessation of it, which was the only way I had experienced bereavement until then – something I most dreaded. Myckie's death was the conclusion of her life and, in spite of my sadness at the loss, I was able to experience fully that process of giving up the attachment to a close person when their life ends. It was as if a part of me was reassured about the quality of a death brought about by nature, rather than through the brutality and violence of other people – those dreaded aspects of human behaviour which were deeply imprinted on my childhood memories. There was something of a quality of holiness in natural death, and I was no longer so desperately frightened of being left alone and helpless. All this contributed to my feeling a special sense of acceptance of Myckie's departure from my life.

Later, during my first year in London, I met the much-loved pianist Dame Myra Hess who had initiated the war-time concert series in London's National Gallery. On hearing that I had been a pupil of Henrietta Michaelson, she told me how much she owed to her. Henrietta had come to London from New York to study with the distinguished teacher Tobias Matthay, with whom Myra was also studying. The two of them became very friendly and some time later, on returning to New York, Henrietta invited Myra to come there and introduced her to a concert agent, through whom Myra developed a highly successful career in the USA. It is not common for a performing artists to assist another in this way.

I was now separated from the quartet, alone as a pianist, and feeling that there was no one I wished to study with after Henrietta's death. During the following year, the scene was set for achieving some resolution to my relationship problems with Gabi. There was increasing tension between us. Gabi was jealous of my going anywhere to perform – he certainly would not accept any shared responsibility for running our house and openly said that I should not expect to continue as a pianist if we had a child. It was this attitude that dug the grave for our marriage.

Our separation came about in a rather convoluted way. During one of the periods when Gabi ceased to talk to me – on this occasion for almost three months – I became involved with a man who wanted me to leave Gabi and marry him. He did all he could to exploit the weaknesses of my relationship with Gabi to ingratiate himself to me. Every unkind gesture on Gabi's part, he counteracted with much caring and thoughtful attention towards me. I found him following me everywhere I went, turning up to collect me from the Music Academy when I finished teaching, and attempting to show every kindness he could think of. Such a lavish display of affection against a background of emotional insensitivity, or even downright hardness on Gabi's part, was understandably an attraction for me. I began to like all this special attention yet, when the moment came for me to say yes to his proposal of marriage – which would mean breaking up his own marriage and leaving behind his two little boys – I could not even contemplate the idea. As much as I enjoyed the relationship that was developing between us, I knew that I could not live with the guilt of causing so much suffering to his wife and children. I have always thought that a person's feelings cannot be accountable to anyone – including parents and spouses – but that we do have to account for our actions. Therefore, it was quite impossible for me to even think of taking a husband from his wife and a father from his children. We were both disappointed and sad. Soon he took up a very interesting post abroad and I began to receive very long letters almost daily. Our correspondence continued for some months. I also received many wonderful gifts, particularly books on music which were then only available in Europe.

Gabi knew nothing of this relationship between me and the man he knew socially very well. But one day, quite unexpectedly, the bombshell exploded. In a large volume of music, which Gabi was returning to the library for me, the librarian found several pages of a letter which she handed back to him.

This was one of the many letters I had received from my friend. It was a distinctly passionate love letter. Gabi was profoundly shaken. He came home looking ashen and stunned. I felt shocked and frightened. I knew that this was the end of our marriage and I felt very confused. Evidently, I must have left the letter in the music volume, as I often received and read them while I was working at the piano. But how strange that I chose to ask Gabi to take that particular volume back to the library for me! Did I subconsciously intend him to find out and put an end to our marriage, which I myself was unable to bring about? I have often wondered about that.

However, the deed was done. There followed a few weeks of acrimonious tension and some typical scenes of outbursts of anger from Gabi (and states of panic on my part). During one such outburst he collected up all the books I had received as presents from my lover, took them into a field near our home, dragging me along by the hand, and set them alight. Our life together had truly come to an end. Infidelity was something absolutely impossible for Gabi to get over. He was quite unable to overcome his shock and anger towards me and, ultimately, I was unwilling to stay under that regime of terror. Having found a place to stay I took my piano, books and personal belongings and left. I moved into the home of some very special friends who knew all about the problems between Gabi and me.

Dr Schossberger and his wife, Stella, were a highly sensitive and remarkable couple who often attended the various musical events at Henrietta Michaelson's house. They knew me well as a pianist and, a little while before the break-up of my marriage, Stella began to come to me for piano lessons. Her husband was one of the leading psychiatrists in Jerusalem and headed a psychiatric hospital there. Dr Schossberger, on hearing from his wife about the distressing situation between Gabi and me, suggested that we both come to him for counselling. Gabi's reaction though, was, 'Why? I am not mad. There is nothing wrong with me. If you need a psychiatrist, that is your affair.' Knowing his unyielding attitudes in all matters of personal relations, such a response was to be expected. However, I felt so shaken by what was going on in our life at that point, that I took up the offer of help and began to have therapy sessions with Dr Schossberger. Only then did I begin to understand how much there was to unravel and to heal from my past. Much of my underlying anxiety began to appear with vivid memories of very stressful episodes from the wartime period of my childhood.

I responded to therapy spontaneously and in the early sessions re-experienced some very harassing scenes from the war along with all the powerful emotions that were bound up in them. Together with that, my separation from Gabi brought about a very painful sense of loneliness. I remember a specific moment: standing one night on the balcony of the house where I was staying and watching the rich star-covered sky, I experienced an almost physical pain in the whole of my being as a great sadness and loneliness overwhelmed me. This was the first time I fully experienced the raw feeling of complete emotional pain. It may have been there years before in Poland when our lives were shattered, Father had disappeared and I was so terrified and helpless but, wildly trying to survive, I may have been unable to fully experience the horror of what was happening around me. Years had passed and once again I found myself without a home, and permanently separated from the person with whom, until that moment, I had shared my life. The only difference was that now my survival was not threatened – I could therefore now feel all that had to be suppressed when suffering separation and loss in my childhood.

At the time of my break-up with Gabi I was due to fulfil my annual engagement with the Radio Symphony Orchestra in Jerusalem. I played Chopin's 'Piano Concerto No. 2 in F Minor' – a work I had loved since first hearing it in Poland. It meant much to me to perform it, yet my emotional state was so disturbed that I was not able to enjoy the occasion and did not play as well as I could. At the time, I felt as if my whole world had crumbled and the magic of music, which previously always gave me a sense of release from the sorrows and dreariness of life, was clouded for me on that occasion by the potency of all I was experiencing at the time. I felt insecure and lost and that undermined even my musical ability. All I wished for was to find some sense of peace, love and security. I was a lost refugee once again and did not know what life had in store for me. My financial situation was very constrained since, during our marriage, Gabi had been the main breadwinner. Within a few months, however, I was offered more teaching at the Jerusalem Music Conservatoire and was able to support myself financially. Also, before our divorce came through, Gabi tried to persuade me to return to him and save our marriage – but it was too late for me. I had lived through the great anguish of separation and could not take a step backwards. I moved into a flat with two other young women and somehow went on with teaching and some practising. I formed a very close friendship with a former colleague from

Myckie's class – Edna. We spent hours together talking about music, art, people, the Israeli situation (always a controversial subject) and, of course, our own private lives.

In the end, the divorce proceedings proved to be quite simple as we both agreed to the separation, made no claim against each other and had no children. After seven years, everything was over with my marriage to Gabi. There was an empty and arid space left in my life. My family in Australia, particularly my mother, wrote letters full of concern. I had to reassure them that it was all for the best.

I became friendly with a young musician called Simcha, from the Radio Symphony Orchestra in Jerusalem. He was a horn player and had come to Palestine from France. Simcha was also a Holocaust survivor with a dramatic childhood. His mother had 'abandoned' him and his older brother at a main railway station in Paris one day, after discovering that all Jews were going to be rounded up and sent for extermination within days. She left the two boys sitting at a table having some refreshments, saying that she was just going away for a few moments. She left them there deliberately, hoping that someone would take pity on them and save them. She knew that her staying with them meant death in a concentration camp for all of them. The two brothers (aged around eight and ten) did survive and, of course, had an incredible story to tell.

Simcha came to see me every day and we began to spend much time together. I went to all the concerts he played in. We spent time with other musicians. We both seemed to have similar burdens of distress from childhood to share. I think this drew us close. We developed a warm though undemanding relationship which alleviated our basic loneliness and gently soothed the real wounds we each nursed inside ourselves.

Part IV

ENGLAND FROM 1960

CHAPTER 21

London – the Alexander Technique

It was during the first summer after my divorce, while I was spending much time with Simcha, that I unexpectedly received a letter from my friend and fellow pianist Ora Nelken, also a former pupil of Henrietta Michaelson. The letter came from London where Ora was studying at the time. She had heard about my divorce and, on the spur of the moment, suggested that I join her in London for a few weeks in order to have some lessons in the Alexander Technique, which she thought I was sure to find wonderful. This invitation was another important landmark in my life, though at the time I had no way of realising its significance for my future.

It so happened that Simcha was also planning to leave Israel and return to Paris – he had grown restless with being an orchestral player and wanted to take on greater challenges in the musical world. Eventually he worked his way to receiving a doctorate in music at the Sorbonne, and undertook most exciting research in, and recording of, traditional

North African music – quite an impressive achievement for one who, as a boy, was left by his mother in such dramatic circumstances.

Having received the letter of invitation to come to London I at first dismissed the idea as an unrealistic fantasy. My income was very modest at the time, even by Israeli standards, and was certainly not enough for me to afford even the cheapest fare to London. But I began to mention to friends the 'impossible' suggestion of my going to London and, to my amazement, various solutions gradually emerged. Someone introduced me to a student travel organiser who offered to give me a student fare even though I wasn't studying any more. This meant that I would travel by the cheapest available transport: a Greek or Turkish boat from Haifa to Marseilles and then a two-day train trip to London; in all, one week's journey. What seemed at first to be quite an impossible proposition began to turn into a feasible reality. But even this extremely cheap form of travel cost more than I could afford. However, one day while in casual conversation with a young woman – a piano teaching colleague – I mentioned that I had been invited to London and even offered a very cheap fare but that it was really out of reach for me. On hearing this, she asked how much money I needed. I told her. She took out her cheque book, made out a cheque in my name for the entire sum, and gave it to me there and then. I was astounded. 'How can I accept this, and when would you want it back?' I asked. She smiled and said, 'Whenever you have enough to pay me'. At that moment, my journey to London was decided.

Simcha, along with some other good friends, also encouraged me to go and helped me to arrange the six-week trip

which I would take in the summer of 1960. The Music
Academy kindly offered to take care of my class of piano
pupils during my absence, so that I should not suffer financially. What I did not know was that I would soon willingly
put myself into a situation of much greater difficulty with
regard to money – or should I say the lack of it – than I
experienced after the breakdown of my marriage.

The cheapest boat proved to be a Turkish passenger ship
whose crew spoke only their native language. The conditions on the boat for those like me, travelling on an especially cheap ticket, were quite unbearable. I had to share a
cabin, which was right next to the engine room, with another
young woman. As we were travelling in August through the
Mediterranean, the combined heat of the Middle East and the
ship's engines left us barely able to breathe, let alone sleep.
We had several days' and nights' journey to get to Marseilles.
After two tortuous sleepless nights in which we applied wet
towels to our faces and bodies to prevent ourselves from
fainting, I discovered that a young woman, whom I had previously briefly met in Gabi's office, was also on this boat and
also going to London. She had a berth in a cabin on the top
deck. As soon as she heard about the conditions I had to put
up with in the bowels of the ship, she insisted that I share her
berth. How we managed to sleep in that small space I cannot
understand, but Ruth and I formed a close friendship on that
journey which has lasted to this day.

Before going on to London I saw Simcha for two days in
Paris. He was at the beginning of his adventure in searching
for some new musical direction in France. This was my third
visit to a European country since our emigration to Israel in

1950. The previous time was an exciting two-month stay in Paris with Uncle Max while I undertook postgraduate study with a French pianist who taught at the École Normale de Musique. During my visit, I once more experienced the great warmth and generosity of Uncle Max, who always related to me as if he were my father. In the light of everything he had done for me from the time of our escape from the ghetto, he definitely played the role of a parent. That visit was the first time I had travelled away from Gabi while we were still married.

At the end of August 1960 I arrived in London with a small suitcase containing enough clothes for a six-week stay. Ora, the friend who had originally suggested the trip, invited me to stay in the small apartment she shared with her future husband, Shmuel Nelken, for the entire six weeks. From the outset of my visit I felt as if London was somewhere I was destined to be. Coincidentally, for quite a number of years before coming to England, I had an occasionally recurring dream of being in very beautiful, green, lush countryside. Only after travelling out of London into the countryside did I recognise the beautiful landscape of my dreams. It was extraordinary, as if I had always known that I would one day be in such surroundings and as if I was always longing for them.

I felt a sense of relief at being in a cooler climate, seeing architecture that dated from before the twentieth century and generally realising how basically European rather than Middle Eastern I was. No wonder there had been such a fundamental difference in conditioning between Gabi and me.

I loved London straightaway and, most of all, I was very profoundly impressed by my first experience of lessons in the

Alexander Technique at the Alexander Foundation. Here, I was very fortunate to be introduced to one of the most outstanding exponents of Alexander's teaching and immediately experienced its extraordinary effects. My impressions of the Technique were so powerful that I instantly felt that I wished to learn as much about it as possible. The man who gave me my first lessons was Patrick Macdonald, the most experienced and long-standing exponent of the Technique, having been a pupil of Alexander from the age of ten (he was 50 when I met him). Even after only a few lessons I experienced a sense of freedom and lightness of movement, of a kind I had never felt before – particularly when playing the piano. For the first time in all my years at the piano, I felt an effortlessness in playing which I would previously not have thought possible. It was that special quality of ease which made me feel I must learn the Technique for longer than just the six weeks I planned to stay in London.

Having found that Patrick Macdonald was starting a course for training teachers of the Alexander Technique, in which he was going to teach a small group of students individually each day, I seized on this as an opportunity for me to have as much instruction from him as I could afford. I enrolled on his teacher training course in October 1960, intending to take just one year of the three-year course as I only wanted to learn for my own benefit and did not intend to become a teacher of the Technique. There was never any question in my mind about doing anything other than music. Whatever else I had to learn to advance my standard as a musician I eagerly undertook. The Alexander Technique seemed to be an enormously valuable aid in my further development as a pianist; that is why it so caught my imagination. With hindsight I know that I was right in thinking so. Learning to follow Alexander's teaching has led me over the years towards knowledge about myself, and others, which has opened up a wealth of new possibilities in piano playing, and given me new insights into some aspects of human behaviour and reactions. I somehow perceived that I had to follow the new path which presented itself to me.

However staying in London proved easier said than done as I only had a six-week visitor's visa for the UK and a very limited amount of money to live on. I had to find a way of earning some money to pay for accommodation and food, as well as for the Alexander course. For the first and only time in my life I resorted to asking my mother for money, in order to pay for one year's tuition on Patrick Macdonald's training course. At the same time, through contact with other Israeli students in London, I was told that the producer of *Hebrew Hour* on the BBC's World Service was looking for a woman to broadcast news in Hebrew and that I should apply. I instantly rejected the suggestion as I didn't think my accent in Hebrew would equal that of an Israeli-born speaker. However, I was persuaded to try a microphone audition and so approached the producer. To my utter surprise he liked my voice for broadcasting and instantly asked me to read editions of Hebrew news two or three times a week. I was paid the equivalent of the cost of a half-week's food for each half-hour broadcast. This was manna from heaven for me. There still remained the essential problem of being allowed to stay in the UK for a whole year. This meant changing my official status from that of 'visitor' to 'student'. Once more a fellow student came to my rescue by introducing me to someone who was able to arrange precisely that change in my visa. I became a student with a special stamp in my passport which stated: 'The bearer of this passport will not undertake any work – paid or unpaid – while resident in the United Kingdom'. I was also asked to teach some basic Hebrew at a synagogue's Sunday school, which helped to add a little to my meagre income. Both the Hebrew broadcasting and the Hebrew teaching, I understood, were not considered UK work.

In my new situation, some very special friends gave me invaluable help and support. These were Adam and Alicia Melamed (later known as 'Adams'); the closest friends of my brother-in-law, Julian and my sister. They had settled in England after the war. Adam, who together with Julian survived the Holocaust hidden by the peasant woman, was now the owner of a small business in London and his wife became a fine painter, under the name Alicia Melamed Adams. On meeting me in London some 15 years after our first acquaintance in Poland in the post-war period, they extended a generous helping hand by giving me a room for an unlimited time in their very small house in London. They were keen to assist me in every possible way. I was particularly amused by Alicia's attempts to find a husband for me – she was always trying to interest me in some young man whom I generally found uninteresting and unattractive, and with whom I had nothing in common except a Jewish background. Even that I found created more of a chasm than a bridge, as my Jewish background was moulded by my childhood in the Holocaust, and by the liberating experience of ten years living and studying in Israel as a young woman. What I found truly touching was Alicia's sensing my passion and dedication to music.

Within my first year of training at the Alexander Foundation I was asked to play a recital at the Ben-Uri Gallery; it was the first time I performed in public in London. Alicia came to the concert and responded so enthusiastically that she immediately wanted to do anything possible to help me. I had at that point acquired a cheap upright piano at an auction. Alicia offered for me to accommodate it in their son's room – the only one in the house with just enough space for it. I offered in return to give the teenage Charles – their only son – some piano lessons, which alas did not bear much fruit as he was not particularly interested in the subject, to the disappointment of us all.

Once I started my first year of training with Patrick Macdonald I realised that to benefit more fully from what I was learning, I needed to continue for at least a further year. When the end of the first year's training approached, I spoke to Mr Macdonald about my desire to continue the training, which, however, was quite beyond my means. I told him that, having considered all the financial options, I came to the conclusion that the only way I could afford to continue my training – which was very important to me – would be to sell the piano I had in Israel. This was my one valuable possession and central to my life as a pianist that I truly cherished, but I now contemplated giving it up for something I was deeply convinced was crucial to my future professional, as well as personal development. Hearing that I was prepared to sell my piano, Mr Macdonald must have realised the extent of my commitment to continuing my training with him – having heard me play in my first concert at the Wigmore Hall not long before, he knew that I was a dedicated, professional pianist. He did not give an immediate response to what I suggested, but said I should leave it with him for a week before making any decisions.

I could not have anticipated the outcome of my conversation with Patrick Macdonald about my situation. He arranged a full scholarship for me to cover my fees, not only for the second year of training, but for the entire remainder of the three-year course. He told me that he had arranged this scholarship from the Chamberlain Foundation on the understanding that I would pay it back when I began working again. I was now set on course to becoming a fully qualified teacher of the Alexander Technique, although I continued to treat the training as only an additional strand in widening my overall education as a pianist.

I feel very grateful for what I received from Patrick Macdonald during the three years of being his student on the teacher training course, as well as in the many additional lessons he gave me from time to time during the years after the completion of my training. The Alexander Technique teaches one a way towards a growing conscious awareness of how one functions and it therefore seems to me to be of paramount importance, especially in the life of an artist.

While training in the Alexander Technique, I found that many questions arose for me about various well-established principles in piano playing. I began to re-examine several ideas widely accepted by pianists and which I had inherited from my excellent piano teachers. The new insight I was gaining from the Alexander Technique pointed towards not accepting any dogmas, even if they came from the most respected people. I began to challenge the assumption that something has to be done in a certain, definite way because it was always done so. Is it necessarily the one true way, or simply the only one I know and am used to? A whole range of questions arose related to that – namely to my attachment to the known, and the habitual, in many aspects of playing and music-making, as well as in other areas of my life. The possibility of seeing oneself and the things one does in more than one way, I have found most enlightening and liberating. I found the Alexander Technique to be a process from which one gains more understanding the longer one engages in it.

When I committed myself to staying in London for one year in order to join the Alexander course, the Music Academy in Jerusalem extended my leave without pay – on the understanding that I would resume my teaching the following year.

I soon made new acquaintances and friends and was invited into English homes. Before coming to England I was told that this would not happen for a long time, because the English were such reserved and private people who did not open their homes to foreign visitors. How strange that this should have been the impression of the English held by many foreigners who had never visited the country. I found, almost immediately, remarkable cordiality, friendliness and warmth of hospitality amongst my new English acquaintances.

Here for the first time I could see on stage the Shakespeare plays I had originally discovered in Polish. The experience of English theatre and the magic of Shakespeare's language worked its spell on me. I could understand the language, purely because of my familiarity with the stories from the time I became captivated as a teenager, reading these great plays in Polish translation. I was often surprised by the cool, sometimes uninterested, responses I met with from some English people when expressing my love and enthusiasm for Shakespeare. Apparently, they could not share my enthusiasm because Shakespeare had been introduced to them at school in a way that precluded any sense of excitement and real discovery.

The many remarkable concerts I was inspired by at this time bring to mind one of the greatest pianists of the twentieth century, Arthur Rubinstein. I hardly ever missed a concert by him from the day I first heard him in Israel when I was in my teens, and continued to hear his remarkable playing each season after moving to London. Rubinstein always had an adoring full audience whenever he played.

Years later, and not long after he had retired from the concert platform, while my husband Roger and I were attending a performance of Mozart's opera Don Giovanni *at Covent Garden, we noticed a distinguished white-haired old man sitting alone in the stalls when the rest of the audience left at the interval. We realised, that it was in fact Arthur Rubinstein. This famous artist, who had been adored by concert audiences around the world, was sitting alone unnoticed by anyone around him. How fickle fame can be! Roger*

encouraged me to go up to him and address him in Polish,
Rubinstein's and my native language. I approached him
and told him I was a pianist and thanked him for the joy,
pleasure and inspiration I had received from his concerts
over many years. He gallantly took my hand, kissed it
and, thanking me, said he was on a visit for a few pleas-
urable days in London from his home in Paris.

We said goodbye and I rejoined Roger and said that
I could now understand the unique beauty of sound that
was so special in Rubinstein's playing. It was to me
obvious from the warmth, vibrancy and sensitivity of his
hand which I felt when he took mine.

Although I loved Israel for many reasons, especially
because of the sense of dignity it restored in me after my
Holocaust experiences, being in England seemed very natural. I felt at home in a European country – and especially so in
London. I find it hard to explain, but it felt as if I was destined
to discover my new path in life in this particular environ-
ment. Indeed, I found there were three important steps along
that new path: the Alexander Technique, psychotherapy and,
a little later, my second marriage. They all happened in that
order, though not smoothly or without numerous difficulties.

CHAPTER 22

Shadows from the Past – Inner Illness

A few months after my coming to London the darkness of fears which had clouded my dreams for years began to come out into my conscious daily life. Not long after starting to train at the Alexander Foundation I had to face one of the most disturbing and painful states that I had experienced until then. This was triggered by my highly fraught relationship with a man I met during the early part of my stay in London. He seemed at first to be a charming, sophisticated, clever person – an Englishman who lectured in philosophy. I liked him and was drawn to him for strange reasons, as if I was subconsciously getting myself into a situation which would inevitably lead to trouble. My greatest desire was to find stability and anchorage in sharing my life with someone, but what I found in that instance was just the opposite. The man turned out to be psychologically sick, though intellectually very clever. Meeting him and becoming intimately involved with him was the last drop in an already full cup of anxieties from my past. Life became so painful that every morning I dreaded having to face another day. I was unable to eat or sleep and began to lose weight at an alarming rate. Life lost all sense and purpose for me. I felt unable to do anything, even to play the piano. Just the thought of playing became quite repugnant to me, and the mere sound of a piano turned into a source of anxiety. Somehow every creative step seemed impossible. I had to reject everything except my training course. Each day I managed to get to my Alexander class and there the work I received from my teacher had the effect of lifting the thick cloud of depression which engulfed me for much of the rest of the time.

However, within an hour or so after leaving the class, the depression returned. Eventually, when I thought that my life was falling apart completely, I wrote to Dr Schossberger in Jerusalem and told him how sick I felt, asking whether I could be hospitalised if I returned to Israel. His reply assured me of every support I might need. In his letter, Dr Schossberger said he was confident that I would get through this difficult patch and recover without having to return to Israel and go into a hospital. He concluded with the story of an earthenware jug which stood by the side of a road bearing an inscription 'I went through fire so that I could hold water for the thirsty traveller'. My dear good friend Dr Schossberger wrote that he believed I would not only recover but, as a result of what I was going through, I would one day be able to help others. His letter was of great importance and support to me. It helped me to find the will to approach a doctor and ask for help.

At the same time, something rather touching happened to me quite unexpectedly. A letter from Paris arrived in which my friend Simcha announced that he had received the sum of £50 which he 'did not need' and was sending it to me. As I had hardly any money at the time, this gift was my only means of getting help from a psychotherapist. There was nothing else I felt could help me to get through what was happening to me. I had to ask for help and I knew that it would have to be psychotherapy. Everything in my life seemed to lie in ruins at that point and it seemed that without some real psychotherapeutic help there was no hope that my life would change, and become worthwhile and creative. There was some deep recess in my psyche which contained overwhelming pain – much of it from the wartime experiences of my childhood. Some of this came to the surface after my divorce from Gabi, but the true intensity of it was unleashed as a result of this abortive relationship with my philosophy lecturer boyfriend. A second separation within the space of a year from a man with whom I had a close relationship put too much strain on my fragile inner stability. All my defences seemed to break down and once more I had to face the raw pain of separation along with the ensuing fear, anxiety and sense of complete helplessness. It is hard to describe the powerful, crushing reality of such a state. By the grace of God a small spark of self-preservation motivated me to seek professional help. Thankfully I found it.

My state of anxiety turned into periods of panic which made me feel almost as if I was drowning. In one such moment, when I felt that I could not cope any longer, I telephoned a very distinguished psychiatrist from London's Tavistock Clinic, whose name had been given to me by another doctor. I had seen him once for a consultation and explained that I had just received a small sum of money which I wanted to use to pay for therapy for as long as it was possible. The psychiatrist asked me various questions to assess my general state and then promised he would find a suitable psychotherapist to take me on. When I telephoned him a week later I was in floods of tears and asking for immediate help, as I felt that I could not bear my state any longer. He then invited me to see him the next day and put me in touch with a younger man who was to become my therapist. I began to go to him twice a week. My most immediate need was some support in coping with the acute anxiety of separation which I had to live through at that time. I was about to leave my mis-chosen boyfriend. While I fully realised that on no account must I stay with him, or else my personal goals would be thwarted, the prospect of experiencing yet another separation, another loss, was causing my severe state of anxiety, panic, sleeplessness and really almost total inability to function. During those months, I could hardly do anything. Certainly, I was quite unable to play and wanted nothing to do with music. It seemed to me at the time that I should never want to play again. One thing was quite clear to me – I did not want to deal with the responsibilities of a musical career. That certainty was how I felt at the time. For a while I did not want to hear music or even to look at a piano.

By the time my worst feelings began to ease, something within me wished to play again but just for my own satisfaction. I began to practise because I felt the need to play and to work towards playing as well as I possibly could. The idea of returning to the struggles of being a professional pianist was unthinkable at that point. All I felt was the need to strive towards further development of my music-making abilities. The awakening of this need was no doubt the first glimmer of inner stability, and a reaching out to active life after many months of severe depression, which engulfed and clouded all aspects of my existence. I began to practise a little and it so happened that within a short time I was approached with a request to give a recital.

When I first began seeing my psychotherapist, it was obvious to him that I was in a very distressed state and needed much support and help in order to recover. He therefore found a very tactful way of generously adjusting the fees per session to enable me to see him three times a week for virtually the same sum as I had been previously paying him for two.

The initial introduction I had to psychotherapy with Dr Schossberger in Jerusalem proved to be most important, in the sense that it led me to realise that if my life seemed too difficult to cope with then maybe the solution was to be found not in changing my external circumstances, but rather in understanding my own reactions to them. It was that idea which prompted me to seek professional help when I found my life so unbearable.

Interestingly, today, after years of professional experience, I find a parallel to this principle in piano playing. When a work of music presents apparent difficulties, a certain change in one's attitude and one's perception of such difficulties may dissolve these obstacles and enable one to give a fluent performance. The circumstances in the piece are not the essential difficulty (with a few exceptions), but rather the player's way of responding to them may be the root of the problem. It is fascinating to observe certain principles manifesting themselves in various areas of our lives, where we can see a reflection of our own psychological and mental make-up determining the way we respond to people, situations and tasks. In recent years, I have come to see more and more of these parallels between my own, as well as other people's, responses to life and to music making.

My original intention of staying in London for only one year to learn the Alexander Technique, and then returning to Jerusalem, gradually changed during that time. There were several reasons for this. I began to realise that one year was not sufficient to learn as much as I had hoped. Another reason was that my therapy was becoming very important to me. Many things began to be clarified and episodes of depression became less frequent and less severe. I could see the light at the end of the tunnel.

CHAPTER 23

Marriage to Roger Clynes

Towards the end of my second year in London I met Roger Clynes, a young English architect who was at that time also quite seriously engaged in music making. He ran a choir and an occasional chamber orchestra and gave various concerts with them in and around London. Once again, an architect came into my life, though he could hardly have been more different from Gabi in his character, personality and cultural background.

I met Roger at the birthday party of a mutual acquaintance. We were drawn to one another from the first glance, though our relationship took a little time to develop. I arrived at the party with my philosopher friend and spotted Roger's face, gentle and sensitive, as soon as we walked into the room. As far as I could tell he took no notice of me when I entered, but I later learned how mistaken I had been in thinking he did not pay any attention to me. During that evening as I was talking to a group of people, telling them an amusing story by Guy de Maupassant, Roger joined us and afterwards started chatting to me. At first, he asked me where I came from – the usual question any English person asked on meeting me. Then, on hearing that I was a pianist, he took the opportunity to get my phone number by asking if I would be interested in rehearsing a piano concerto with the orchestra he was working with at the time. That was how he was able to contact me two weeks later. Answering his phone call, I immediately thought he was going to invite me to an orchestral rehearsal but, to my surprise, he asked me to go with him to see an opera at Covent Garden. I accepted the invitation still naively thinking that it was simply a friendly gesture on the part of this nice Englishman, not realising that this was the first step on a road that was to lead to our life together. The opera was Richard Strauss's *Silent Woman*. This title has often been a source of amusing anecdotes about our relationship. Friends who know that I hardly aspire to the reputation of a 'silent woman' have found it comical that my first date with Roger should have been at that particular opera.

Many things were happening in my life at the time Roger and I met. My relationship with the philosophy lecturer was obviously no longer tenable and was on the brink of breaking up. The Alexander training was very intense and was having a powerful effect on me. At the same time my psychotherapy began to reach deeper and I began to see possibilities of gradual changes occurring and healing of some of the old wounds. I often spent hours crying and feeling an overwhelming sadness and sense of loss, but very gradually these spells became a little less frequent. The possibility of playing the piano again became real although definitely not in concerts, which I still did not want to have anything to do with.

However, my playing became the answer to an inner need to make music and to reach out for increasingly finer quality and further ability as a pianist. Once again, playing the piano revealed itself – as it had always done since my childhood – to be an absolute necessity in my life. Gradually I was able to disassociate it from feelings of panic and depression, and liberate it to express the music.

My life in London in the early sixties was fraught with financial insecurity, often bordering on real poverty. Another fact contributed to that (often intense) feeling of insecurity, and that was my not having a permanent home, something I deeply longed for. A part of me was always yearning to have a home of my own. This longing stayed with me for years following the destruction of my parental home during the war. It seemed as if I was aiming and waiting for the return of a HOME. What that really meant I am not quite sure, but it had something to do with bringing about a healing from past hurts – a re-affirming of one's place in life, where warmth and affection exist; somewhere to sense one's roots firmly established. My childhood left me with a restless existence. Coming to live in Israel was only a partial answer to that feeling of being permanently uprooted. Israel gave me back my right to exist as a human being on equal terms with any other person, be he or she 'Aryan' or of some other invented description. Yet it did not fulfil that deep longing for a permanent, personal HOME. Only now can I understand it more clearly. For years I had unconsciously looked for my father and the home of my childhood. It constituted a central theme in my life's direction, woven together with the deep need to make music.

The years of training to become a teacher of the Alexander Technique were a time of intensive changes. The Technique and psychotherapy proved to be quite parallel roads towards unravelling set patterns in my whole self and in my way of thinking. Both processes, though often uncomfortable, were liberating as well as revealing and educational. I came to see that one may possess education, information and knowledge, but without acquiring some means of self-knowledge, one is frequently building castles in the air, living largely in states of illusion about oneself and others. In my case there is no question that, had it not been for the support, as well as the insights into my conditioning, which I received from psychotherapy, I would not have been able to function, either in my personal life or as a pianist. And, had it not been for the changes in, as well as new understanding of, how my total co-ordination of mind, body and psyche could be brought into better balance, my development as an artist and as a teacher would no doubt have been vastly more limited. I feel a deep gratitude to providence for having found these re-educating ways which have given me important new perspectives in my life.

I also feel truly grateful to a number of special people without whose help I would not have found out about the existence of these roads to inner growth. Such people either indirectly or directly helped me on the way. There was Henrietta Michaelson; Dr Schossberger; my remarkable Alexander teacher, Patrick Macdonald; and my first therapist in London, Peter Hildebrand. Then there were various people, fellow travellers on the road, whose struggles supported and encouraged my own. Roger, my second husband, who joined me with his support and kindness, without which

I might not have been able to do much of what I did manage to achieve, particularly in my professional life. Of course, through our relationship much else came about that enriched both our lives; the greatest of all was of course the gift of our child, Daniela, who was born some three years after I completed my formal Alexander studies. She brought great joy and fulfilment into our lives.

The birth of Daniela marked a brand new phase for Roger and me. She, naturally, became the centre of our life. During her early childhood, I did not have a very intensive professional life – though I did play and learn new repertoire all the time, gave a few concerts and did some teaching. Because I felt I wanted to be with my child as much as possible it seemed right at the time not to have to go away and play recitals in various places.

As Daniela was growing up she began to show signs of real musicality. From her early years she loved to sing, starting with various childhood songs. In her teens her interest in singing grew more and more and she began to develop a very lovely voice. Our house was often filled with the sounds of the recordings of singers such as Barbra Streisand, Cleo Laine and others. After finishing school she received a scholarship to study jazz music at the Guildhall School of Music and Drama. This led to her becoming a professional jazz singer and teacher. The quality of her voice is often commented on, such as in one review which describes it as 'an angelic voice'. Daniela entering the music profession seems to prove the saying that 'the apple doesn't fall far from the tree'!

The work on my own playing, however, went on. I was gradually attempting to incorporate into piano playing what

I had learned in my Alexander training. This proved initially to be a vast and difficult task. It has to do with the changing of many habitual aspects of playing and replacing them with more consciously directed ways. I found it challenging but at the same time very fascinating. It was a journey on a hitherto unknown path in piano playing which I undertook quite alone. None of the established methods pointed in that direction. Sometimes when doubts assailed me in my work there was no one in the music community I could turn to for help or reassurance in what I was hoping to achieve. However, the experience and understanding I received from the Alexander Technique kept me convinced that the new possibilities in playing which I was working towards did indeed exist. This also later led to my giving piano courses dealing specifically with this approach to playing.

Just as my work in piano playing took on a steady direction of new development, so also in my personal existence a slow gentle change was taking place. The very severe states of anxiety gave way to a somewhat quieter emotional state. I was able to see more the often irrational causes of anxiety and so to lessen its influence on my way of living. Naturally, having a child sometimes brought worries to stir up inner fears and disquiet, but I was able to meet these and deal with them far better than I had in the past.

For some time after I married Roger, made my home with him in London and had Daniela, I had hardly any professional work. I was learning more about music and piano playing but I had no pupils and gave no concerts. There was one period which was an exception, but then I had just a few pupils; none of them were professional music students and therefore they could not work with the kind of intensive attention that I believe is necessary in the pursuit of excellence and the perfecting of one's abilities. I did though acquire several friends from amongst those people who studied with me. For a number of years after Daniela's birth I felt professionally isolated with no connection to any major music institution.

Finally, in a rather roundabout and unexpected way, things began to change. A young, highly intelligent woman who attended a short course I gave in the Alexander Technique, became so intrigued by what I taught that she turned round one day and said 'You must be a very good piano teacher'. I laughed and replied that I did think I probably was. This young student, Jenny, who had just graduated in music from Edinburgh University, began to have piano lessons with me. She was also doing a course in music therapy at the Guildhall School of Music & Drama. She enthused about her private piano teacher to a colleague, who repeated Jenny's stories about my methods of teaching to her own teacher at the Guildhall. That teacher became intrigued by what she heard, contacted me for some lessons and introduced me to yet another piano teacher – Carola Grindea – who, on hearing me play in a recital at London's Purcell Room and knowing about my experience in the Alexander Technique, asked me 'Why don't you teach at the Guildhall School of Music?' I laughed and replied 'I really don't know why I don't teach there!' Carola spoke of me to Alan Percival, the then Principal of the School. He invited me to meet him and immediately asked me to join the teaching staff of the piano department. I was to introduce the Alexander Technique and its relevance to piano playing as a new subject for the students of that department. What a chain of connections!

Soon after that Carola and I became very friendly and one day she asked me to join her in founding a committee for her 'brainchild': a European Piano Teachers' Association (EPTA), modelled on the one then existing for string players. It has since become a hugely active and popular international association.

From then on, however, I came into my own as a teacher. I came into contact with the mainstream of young music students, something I have always found exciting, challenging and stimulating. My training and qualification in the Alexander Technique enabled me to give special courses to young pianists. These courses have always aimed towards furthering possibilities of ease in playing and increased sensitivity to musical sonority and expressive qualities. The students and I have always found that the search for those qualities was a way of not only professional but also personal development. Imperceptibly, a certain change in priorities gradually began to take place in my pianistic endeavours. From trying to learn everything I could to aid my successful development as a pianist, I began to learn from the processes involved in that development; certain things which enriched my own personal growth. And so, from having come to the Alexander Technique in order to improve my playing I began to benefit from it as a person. The direction my work has taken has given me many new insights, not only into music but also into other areas of life. What I find especially gratifying is that it leads me continually towards new understanding.

Naturally, my teaching ability was largely the result of what I came to know as a player. The preparation of music for performance and the experience of giving concerts broadened my perspective on the art of music making as a pianist.

Not long after starting to teach regular piano courses at the Guildhall School of Music, I also began to give short summer courses there. Their theme was the introduction of principles of the Alexander Technique and their relevance to music study and piano playing. This subject had never before been taught and was quite unknown in the field of music education in the seventies. The courses began to attract advanced piano students as well as young performers and some piano teachers. Word about my work in this field began to spread. Pianists who attended my summer courses discovered the Alexander Technique and found it to be increasingly helpful in their work. A number of players decided to follow up the summer courses by having further lessons. In fact, I was encouraged to organise short 'refresher' courses during the winter breaks in the academic year. This eventually led to the establishment of the ongoing biannual one-week international courses that I eventually transferred out of the Guildhall School to my own studio. For some years now, these courses have been known as 'Piano Playing with the Alexander Technique'.

The popularity of these courses led to the establishment of a Scholarship Trust founded by past students and friends to enable impecunious talented young pianists to take advantage of these intensive piano study weeks. The trustees decided to name it: 'The Nelly Ben-Or Scholarship Trust'. And the eminent conductor Sir Colin Davis, whose experience and great appreciation of the Alexander Technique for musicians was well known, agreed to become the founding patron of the Trust. By now there have been many recipients of scholarships from the Trust, pianists and students both from the UK and many other countries. Some of them were enabled to come more than once to the courses and so build on what they had learned the previous times. I do feel that my debt to all those who assisted me in my own professional development has been partly paid towards the new generation.

Interestingly, the circumstances of my life brought about a gradual increase in my activities as a pianist parallel to those in teaching. As our little daughter was growing up I found myself being asked to play more as well as to do more teaching. Throughout the years I have been reaching out for a direction which would bring a deeper, subtler quality into both my work and my life. Often I realise how fortunate one is to be able to spend one's energies in the pursuit of personal development and in working on whatever gift one has come into this life with. In my case, although there have been various difficulties, this way of working has enriched my life and added great value to my work in music.

Some 30 years after the loss of my father – a loss which I never allowed myself to experience, think about or speak about – it caught up with me in another painful moment of my life. I was expecting a second child, and was very happy that little Daniela would have a sibling. It was a warm summer and we were spending a few days in a peaceful country cottage nourished by the beauty of the views and tranquillity of the countryside around us. Quite unexpectedly I developed flu symptoms, so we returned home. Next morning

I awoke from a distressing dream in which I was showing some friends what looked like a passport. On the pages of it were photographs of various people. In the middle of the passport was just one large photograph of an open grave in which my father lay. I began to cry in pain, saying to the people near me, 'Look what they did to him!'

Still with the feeling of the pain of pity and loss, I woke up to find that I was beginning to miscarry my pregnancy. The present loss finally triggered the pain of the great loss of my childhood – so deeply hidden from my awareness until that moment. It was at that point, having become seriously ill, that I felt the full impact of both losses: my father and the eagerly awaited child.

CHAPTER 24

Confronting the Past

———⌘———

Giving concerts led to, among other events, my co-oper-
ation with the actor Gabriel Woolf, whose radio perfor-
mances had impressed me greatly. At my suggestion, we
created a programme about the life of Chopin based on
his correspondence and diaries, and those of people close
to him, as well as a selection of some of his finest compo-
sitions ranging from those of his youth to those composed
in his creative maturity. The programme was received
with great enthusiasm by audiences and critics. We per-
formed it several times in London: at the Wigmore Hall,
the Purcell Room and in many venues in England,
Scotland and Wales. Later we were invited to perform
this programme in the USA. On many occasions, we
were asked if we would devise another programme of
a similar character. This we did. It combined works of
the English Romantic poets with the complete Schubert

'Impromptus' and Schumann's 'Kreisleriana'. We gave it the title 'A Celebration of the Romantic'.

In parallel with those unusual concerts involving the spoken word as well as piano music, I continued to play in solo recitals and also performed for the BBC. After hearing my recital at the Queen Elizabeth Hall, the Head of Meridian Records invited me to record a programme of Variations *by a range of composers. This was the first of a number of recordings I made for Meridian, both solo and in chamber music. Giving concerts often led to my being approached by younger pianists for lessons, which created an ongoing strand in my musical life of teaching as well as playing concerts. Looking back, I realise how these two aspects of my musical activities became integrated: teaching further informed my playing, while playing enriched my ability in teaching.*

———❧———

There were moments in my musical life which remain particularly in my memory for reasons other than musical. Two such spring to mind, both partly relating to my Holocaust past.

I was invited, by a highly acclaimed German pianist, Edith Picht-Axenfeld, who taught at the Freiburg Hochschule für Musik, to give classes to the piano students there. It was to be the first time ever that I would travel to Germany. After giving it much thought and discussing it with Roger, I decided to accept the invitation. I felt that by going to the country from which so much tragedy had been brought to the Jewish people, I would finally come face to face with all the residual negative feelings towards Germans that I had harboured from my childhood. We decided to travel together with our three-year-old daughter who would be in Roger's care while I was teaching. We travelled through France by car. At the border crossing to Germany I was suddenly confronted with the sight of a man in a German uniform. It was the same colour that I was in such dread of during the war in Poland. I stopped Roger and exclaimed, 'Look, a German uniform!'. I must have looked so frightened that Roger stopped the car and wanted us to turn back and not proceed with the journey. But at this point I said to him that I must get through this reaction and face post-war Germany to help heal my inner wounds. So we went into Germany. I was cordially received at the Hochschule für Musik (the equivalent of an academy of music in the UK) and Edith Picht could not have been more welcoming. The students were very keen to learn something new from a guest teacher; many of them were postgraduates and showed particular curiosity about me personally. My name, to begin with, 'Ben-Or, where was that from?'

'Israel', I replied.

'Were you born there?'

'No.'

'Where were you born and when did you go to live in Israel?'

'Poland, and 1950.'

'And where were you before that?'

'In Poland.'

And so followed a flood of questions about how I had survived as a Jew in Poland during the war... and so on. I had previously made up my mind that, as I had agreed to come and teach in Germany, I would not speak about my past to anyone. What could I have said that would not be offensive and most hurtful? But the students confronted me with a virtual avalanche of questions about wartime events in Poland, with such a hunger for information from a firsthand witness, that there was no way for me not to answer as truly as I could. What was most poignant was that they had been told nothing by their elders, 'We knew nothing of that...' was the standard response of their parents' generation.

I became acutely aware of the guilt these young people felt for something they were not in the least responsible for, but felt as if they were. They had lost trust in their parents' generation and felt they had not been told the truth about the parents' past. They wished to be free of this terrible stigma of being the sons and daughters of that generation of 'insane perpetrators of untold atrocities'. Among these young German students were a number who had been to Israel. I realised that their journeys to the Jewish state were for them a search for an understanding of their immediate past and a means of fulfilling some deep longing for expiation. In my encounters with the sincerity of these young people's longing for explanations and absolution from the sins of their predecessors, I sensed their shame and pain and felt great pity for them.

Guilt can arise from feelings that often have no logical explanation. For many years after the war such feelings had plagued me. From time to time they would re-surface in my questioning the fact that I survived, while six million other

Jewish people perished. It remains an unanswerable, disturbing question.

During this two-week teaching spell in Freiburg, Edith Picht arranged for us to stay in a guest house in the Black Forest near Freiburg. One evening, on returning from teaching, I found on my bed a beautifully bound book about Felix Mendelssohn. On questioning the receptionist about the book, which I thought had been left there by mistake, we were told it had been left for me by Baron von Mendelssohn who lived in an adjacent villa. I then saw there was also a small card inscribed, 'With compliments, Baron von Mendelssohn.' It then transpired that the Baron was a direct descendant of the great composer. On hearing that a pianist from England was a visiting teacher in Freiburg, he showed interest in meeting me, as he had studied in England in his youth. We were invited to the Baron's home and told the incredible story of how he managed to avoid persecution by the Nazis, who might have considered him to be of Jewish descent, even though Felix Mendelssohn had died more than a hundred years earlier and was certainly brought up as a Christian by his father, a religious convert, in the early nineteenth century. The Baron owned a set of the most beautiful drawings made by Felix Mendelssohn during a journey in Switzerland in 1842. These he kept hidden in a bank vault during the Nazi years. After the war, the Baron produced a limited number of bound copies of these drawings and gave the originals to a Berlin museum. Having met us, the Baron generously gave me six copies of these precious, remarkable sets of drawings of Swiss scenery, stipulating that I should give some to musicians I felt deserved to be owners of such a gift.

I was most touched and excited by this encounter. A number of years later, while doing some guest teaching in Leipzig, the home of Felix Mendelssohn and the centre of much of his musical activities, I was shown the famous Church of St Thomas in which Bach had officiated for many years. The Church traditionally installed windows with stained glass images of the famous composers associated with it or generally admired. One of these was of Felix Mendelssohn. The Nazis removed Mendelssohn's stained glass image because, although a Christian, he was the grandson of a highly valued and respected Jewish philosopher, Moses Mendelssohn. It was reinstated after the war.

My later contact with Germany was through a very talented young pianist on a postgraduate course at the Guildhall School of Music, who met me while taking part in my classes there. After leaving the Guildhall School she continued to have periodic lessons with me for years. I felt warmly about her and was interested in giving her as much as could be of benefit to her. She came to know about my childhood and on one occasion almost tearfully said how moved she was that I could be so friendly to her despite my background. It was in a moment such as this that I could fully sense the weight of guilt borne by the post-war generation of Germany's young, especially sensitive, people.

CHAPTER 25

Various Journeys

On occasions, when intensely engaged in some performing and teaching activities I recall what background
my present life sprang from and reflect on how miraculous
life can be, and how mysterious its paths. When I look back
at my first few years in London, being almost penniless, trying to study and sustain myself somehow in a vast foreign
city against all the odds, I wonder where I got my strong
impulse to find a way to achieve what I so wished for? There
were so many practical and psychological difficulties I had to
deal with. Now, from the position of a longer experience of
life it seems quite hard to believe that I was able to cope with
such challenges – all of them resulting from the abnormal
stresses of a Holocaust childhood. I can only feel a humbling
sense of gratitude to providence and to all the people who
extended their help in so many different ways. Without them
I could not have done any of the things I have managed to
do. These days when some young people who come to study
with me feel that I am useful in furthering their development,

I experience a joy in feeling that what I had to struggle with and overcome was not only for my own benefit, but could also pave a way for others to follow. There is a Hebrew proverb saying 'I have been educated by all my pupils'. This is certainly borne out by my experience of the process of teaching and playing – both, to my understanding, are really processes of learning. So it seems is every real encounter between people. Having survived the Holocaust by the grace of God it was incumbent on me to try to learn from the experience, and to go on learning and sharing whatever developed within me, much of it through the depth of the inner language of music.

I have been separated by continents from my closest family – my mother and my sister with her husband, two daughters and a son. Staying in London after the completion of my studies, marrying Roger, establishing a home and family (small though it was) meant that my new roots grew into the English soil. I have always felt at ease in England, even though at times some of the differences in temperament between me and those from a similar background on the one hand, and some English people on the other, I have found a little frustrating. But that was never too big a price to pay for living amongst people as civilised and tolerant as the English. Undoubtedly, in many ways I always will remain a foreigner in England – I only need to say 'Hello' on the phone for an English person to ask 'Where do you come from'? At the same time, however, English has become for me the language in which I feel most free to express my thoughts. My day-to-day way of life is quite integrated into the ways of this country. When, occasionally, I wonder where my roots are I feel that some of the deepest ones are without doubt in England. Though I do also feel a very special closeness and affinity with Israel, as well as something of a love/hate sentiment for the Poland of my childhood and early teens.

No doubt a major factor in my integration into life in England was, of course, my marriage to an Englishman and having a child born in that country. The contrast between this long-lasting ongoing marriage to a non-Jewish Englishman and that of my first marriage to a Jew born in Palestine could not be more marked.

In the years during which my work grew to encompass the integration of the ideas and practice of the Alexander Technique into piano playing, I gradually began to be in demand as a teacher of more advanced students and also some very good young professional players and teachers. This led to getting invitations to give concerts and courses in various music schools and university music departments in different countries. Such visits gave me the opportunity to form friendships with people geographically distant. I have made contacts with musicians and non-musicians in countries as far apart as Canada and New Zealand, Hong Kong and Iceland, Mexico and India, and on many visits to the USA. I have met some very special, interesting individuals.

The British Council sponsored two tours for me in response to invitations to give recitals and master classes in Canada and India. The Canada visit was my first time in that country. Travelling from Ottawa where I gave a recital and taught a class at the university through to Kingston, on Lake Ontario – again to play and teach; then on to Nova Scotia, where at Acadia University I fulfilled similar engagements.

We covered many stretches of the journey by car, with Roger driving. This gave us the opportunity to see and experience the vast spaces of the Canadian landscape. For us Europeans it was something never experienced before. The absence of the interfering human hand, together with the majesty and power of this natural world, cast a spell on us. Some years later I taught each spring and late autumn in Toronto, and there in the Art Gallery of Ontario I discovered the wonderfully original paintings by the so-called 'Group of Seven'. These Canadian artists gave vent to their creative originality by breaking completely with the painting language and techniques of Europe to express their own vision of the riches of shapes, colours and atmosphere of the vastness of their homeland. On my many visits to Toronto I taught students and teachers of the Alexander Technique and gave classes to musicians, dealing with many aspects of music making.

My performing and teaching visit to India proved a most fascinating time in my musical life. Again Roger joined me on that trip – our daughter was by then grown up and independent. The first shock for me was at our first port of call on this journey: the city then known as Calcutta. Nothing could have prepared us for what we saw. This was not simply poverty – it was complete desolation. For me, seeing humans living in the streets, deprived of even the most basic shelter sparked memories of the ghetto in Poland. The difference was only in the fact that the ghetto inhabitants were put there by force and as a step towards extermination, whereas the people of Calcutta were abandoned by humanity to their desolate fate. We chose to stay in a very simple dwelling called a Mission, in which we had a small room with a concrete floor, a bed and small table with two wooden chairs. We did, however, have running water through a pipe which acted as a primitive shower. Looking out of our window we saw scores of people lying on the muddy street, each covered by a simple cloth; we could see rats running over the sleeping humans. I found it impossible to fall asleep in the comparative luxury of even the primitive bed in our room. What I saw on the pavements of Calcutta haunted me virtually throughout our four weeks in India, and for a long while after.

There were, however, many other wonderful experiences which were memorable. Most interesting was meeting the teachers and students of the Calcutta School of Music. Those studying Western music, which is so different from the indigenous old and highly complex music of India, I found to be sensitively responsive to the Western musical language. It was a pleasure to work with the students and guide them towards a stylistic understanding of the character of music by composers such as Beethoven, Brahms and Mozart, in whom they were so interested. In my concert in Calcutta I included, amongst pieces by classical composers, music by a contemporary English composer, William Kinghorn, whom I knew personally. (William Kinghorn later wrote and dedicated to me a piano sonata which I recorded and broadcast, and a piano concerto of which I gave the first performance with the orchestra of Leeds College of Music in Leeds Town Hall.) To my surprise the response to this music, in a style no one would have previously heard in India, was extremely positive and excited.

On one occasion during the days I worked in Calcutta, Roger and I were invited to a concert of an unusual quality. This was given by a string orchestra performing the music of Mozart. The players were all teenage boys who had been rescued from a life on the streets by an English monk who was passionate about string playing. He created a home in which the boys received food, clothing and general and musical education, each learning to play a stringed instrument to the level that enabled them to join an orchestra led by the monk. Their playing reached a surprisingly developed standard, considering the deprived background they came from. We were told that the monk who had created this unusual ensemble managed to get financial support for his special venture by bringing the group annually to Europe to give fundraising concerts which were supported by generous donations. It was this continuous financial support of European donors that enabled the flourishing of this remarkable monk's programme.

My India tour continued with a concert in Delhi and again teaching classes to young students of Western music. I was naturally very interested to hear some classical Indian musicians playing Indian music. As it happened it was only after we left Calcutta, the home of the great Indian musician Ravi Shankar, so admired in England, that I learned of the unusual local custom of calling on a musician at his home to be treated to the music he plays. I could have contacted Ravi Shankar and been given a private concert by him in his home, had I been told about such a possibility while in Calcutta, but alas I discovered that too late. However, while in Delhi I asked the music teacher in charge of all my work commitments in the Music School if I could hear some serious Indian music. She made a special arrangement for Roger and me to visit a local, much-admired musician. We were received in the home of a woman who had years of experience, from childhood, of playing and singing according to a long-held oral tradition passed down through generations. We spent several hours listening to her remarkable playing on a multi-stringed instrument called the *viveenana*, as well as to her singing. I asked her some theoretical questions about her musical language and told her something of the theory of Western harmony, which was quite unknown to her. It was only a short exchange on a subject so rich and fascinating on both sides, which could otherwise have taken a long time for us to learn about. It was, however, most interesting and gratifying to have at least that special meeting of such diverse musical cultures.

When the musical part of my visit to India was concluded, we spent more time travelling through the country, going as far as Rajastan. The sights we saw would warrant reams of tales and descriptions not possible in the context of this memoir. I only wish to add that this trip was a profound eye-opening experience of a part of the world, with its ancient sights and sounds, that we could not have imagined.

A few years later, a 19-year-old piano student from Mexico, Ricardo Miranda, came during the summer break to have some piano lessons with me. He proved to be musically gifted, highly intelligent and very mature for his age. It was interesting to work with him that summer. To my surprise, on leaving England to return and continue his studies at home in Mexico City, he asked if I would be willing to go there and teach a course to a group of students he knew. I agreed to go if it could be arranged, although I did not expect that this young man could succeed in setting in motion such a project. I was quite wrong. Ricardo assembled a group of piano students he knew from his music school, as well as two private piano teachers, to cover the expenses of bringing me out to Mexico City during the Christmas holidays to give them a course in piano playing, and to introduce them to some principles of the teaching of Alexander. Roger joined me on this trip which took place shortly after a major earthquake there. We visited some fascinating sites in Mexico City, Teotihuacan and other places nearby. Ricardo proved to be a guide who knew much about his country's history and cultural heritage. The teaching I did was assisted by Ricardo translating much of what I was saying into Spanish for those students whose knowledge of English was limited. As well as being interesting, my time there was productive in relation to the students' work, as I later learned from Ricardo. It also produced another result, namely that Ricardo decided to continue his studies in London and spend six years as my piano student, as well as enrolling on a music programme at London's City University, where eventually he gained a PhD in music. After returning to Mexico he was offered a highly responsible post in his country's Ministry of Culture, taking charge of all its musical institutions and events. It was on reaching this position that he invited me for an extended visit during which I played a recital, gave a piano and Alexander Technique course at the National Conservatory and sat on the jury of a national piano competition. Every aspect of that trip I found very enriching, whether it was performing or giving masterclasses, and also seeing some fascinating sights:

the murals of Diego Rivera; the home he had once shared with his lover, Frida Kahlo and her artistic creations; the house of the architect Luis Barragan; and, finally, a splendid trip to Yucatan. There, a local professor of archaeology showed us round and explained to us the inspiring remains of the ancient culture of the indigenous inhabitants of that land, which were shrouded in mystery and mysticism. What an amazing part of our world!

Returning to the familiarity of our life in England seemed, at the time, as if we had left a place of magic and mystery to come down to earth. However, a year later I was invited back to Mexico as guest chair on the jury of another National Piano Competition. This time I also recorded a CD of 18 mazurkas by three composers – one Mexican and two from Poland: Emanuel Ponce, Frederic Chopin and Karol Szymanowski. This came about as a result of an enthusiastic response to the recital in which I had played six Chopin mazurkas. I was then told that a Mexican composer had also written mazurkas and that the recording company wanted to combine a programme of mazurkas from the two countries. Of course the origin of the mazurka is a Polish folk dance called 'mazurek'. The CD will continue to be a legacy of my contact with Mexico, its music and its wealth of ancient and new art – both very colourful and fascinating.

My work has also taken me to European countries, with Holland a frequent port of call. There I performed at the Recital Hall of the Concertgebouw – the main concert hall in Amsterdam – and on a number of occasions recorded broadcast recitals for Radio Hilversum. I gave masterclasses to piano students at the conservatoires in Amsterdam and Rotterdam on piano playing with the Alexander Technique. Cora Canne-Meijer, the distinguished Dutch mezzo-sporano, having come to one of my masterclasses, realised that the Alexander Technique would be equally relevant to her approach to teaching singing. She therefore invited me to join her at the annual masterclasses she gave to singers in her studio. This arrangement lasted for twenty years until her retirement and she and I have remained close friends since. Some very talented Dutch pianists have come to study with me at different times. I have a special affection for that country and its people, with their warmth, directness and lack of pretentiousness.

Contact with my family in Australia of necessity had to be by correspondence. For many years Mother and I wrote to each other regularly once a week. One of the most touching and painful moments I experienced was after my mother's death while clearing her apartment in Melbourne, together with my sister and Mother's sister Marysia. We found an entire suitcase full of letters I had written to her in over 20 years of our living so far apart. Only at that point did I fully perceive the sadness of her life with its brave struggles, hardships and frustrations; a life filled with longing and an anguished sense of separation from a daughter whom she saved so unselfishly and to whom she was perhaps more attached than to anyone else.

My mother died in 1974 in circumstances which were particularly difficult for me. She had to have surgery and telephoned me from Melbourne to ask me to come and be with her just before her going into hospital. Her call was totally unexpected, even more so her request for me to come to Melbourne. In all the years of our living on two distant continents, Mother had called me only once before and that was on my wedding day in London. At that time she could not afford the journey to come to the wedding.

At the time of my mother's call asking me to come to Melbourne, I was due to play a concert in London's St John's, Smith Square Concert Hall. The posters advertising the programme that I shared with a violinist in some joint works, as well as playing solo, were on display throughout the city. I could have flown to Melbourne for two days and travelled back almost literally onto the concert platform. Consulting two very experienced doctors we knew well I was told that the operation my mother had to undergo was, in their words, 'safer than crossing the road', and that it would be much more helpful to her if I were to spend a longer time with her afterwards, while she was recovering. Mother, on hearing about my commitment to the concert date and therefore my inability to be with her prior to her going into hospital, except for only two days, also agreed that I should come after fulfilling my concert engagement and immediately after the operation. I was planning to bring our young daughter with me and spend some weeks with Mother then.

She was, after all, surrounded by close family – my sister and her own family were nearby, as was Aunt Marysia, along with her husband and daughter – all absolutely devoted to Mother. However, she must have intuitively perceived that we might never meet again, which is why she initially wanted to see me before her operation. Alas her intuition was proved right. As it happened, she died while under the anaesthetic, never regaining consciousness. My feelings on receiving the news about her unexpected death are hard to describe. Not only was there first the shock of losing such a central figure in my life but, as with my father, having to face the loss without actually being there when it happened. The immediate burial, which is the law in Jewish tradition, meant that I was not even able to get to Melbourne for my mother's funeral. The extraordinary way of being parted from both my parents, without the opportunity to be present at the ritual of their burial (and in the case of my father not even knowing the place, time or manner of his death), has left me with a sense of inexplicable helplessness in the face of such a fate.

I was deeply moved, however, when my Rabbi again showed special sensitivity when arranging prayers for my mother in our home. He linked them with the memory of my father's tragic death during the Holocaust, for which I had never before been able to say prayers. Thus a haunting ghost was laid to rest.

After Mother's death, I found not only the hundreds of letters she had received from me over the years but also various papers relating to our past. One of them, which I only read after returning to London, was a statement signed in a Polish court by a person who knew of my father's fate after he was taken from the ghetto – the document describes him being taken to the horrific Janowski prison in Lwów and there executed.

As I mentioned before, I had never been told anything about this. However, even that moment of reading it served as a belated bereavement ritual, which in the case of my father I had never gone through. It seems that some of the age-old customs dealing with mourning, which different societies have evolved, have much practical psychological wisdom in them. They must surely be based on a very deep knowledge of the inner processes of grief. In the Jewish tradition, for instance, there is a specified period of seven days for sitting (as it is called) in mourning. Without my realising it at the time that was exactly what occurred to me after my hearing of Mother's death. Quite spontaneously I simply ceased every occupation and withdrew from all my daily tasks and from any contact with all but my immediate family. I felt totally unable to do anything – not even to answer the door, the phone, or to prepare any food. All I could barely do was just dress in the morning and sit in the house in a state of complete inactivity and numbness. This lasted for precisely seven days. Quite without my intending it or knowing that exactly that amount of time had passed, I got up one morning and began the day with my normal activities. The process I had experienced was complete and I could return to the mainstream of my life again. There is indeed profound wisdom in certain time-honoured traditions – and the Jewish formal mourning over seven days must surely be one of them.

CHAPTER 26

Reflections

Looking back at the different phases of my life from child-hood onwards, it occasionally seems like a collection of various lives strung together by the thread of music running through them – the one uninterrupted thread of inner neces-sity towards a growing need for knowledge of one's real self. This is certainly an enormous question and the longer one asks it the larger it becomes. But even some inkling of an answer brings with it the shattering of certain fantasies and illusions about oneself. This may be upsetting at times but it is certainly enlightening. I do not mean to say that I enjoy futile introspection, but rather a quest for understanding some things about myself that could in fact prove to be of practical use in my life in general and in my musical life too. To understand some of the wealth of patterns which govern one's responses to different challenges and tasks in life does shed light on one's path. It enriches one's ways of living and working. Nowhere have I found that kind of knowledge of more benefit than in my playing and, of course, teaching.

Knowledge (limited as it may be) of oneself helps one to see others with a degree of understanding which goes beyond the usual assumptions we make about people. Dispelling at least some illusions about oneself, and therefore also about others, does bring some clarity into one's life. Perhaps all this has made teaching a fascinating pursuit for me – the process of teaching is an extension of learning. It means finding out, clarifying and searching. Through the pupil's attempt to learn, the teacher has to understand the process as deeply as possible and that, of course, educates the teacher. One thing is unquestionable – there is much to work for in my profession which fires my enthusiasm and my continuing interest in it.

At times when reflecting on the diversity of experiences of my past, I myself find it difficult to believe that they could all have occurred in one person's life. There is no doubt in my mind that I live with deep scars left by a war-torn childhood and, indeed, the events of those times are stored in my memory. However, I also have the wonderful strand of music which stayed within me through the darkest hours and remained as a central driving force over the years. For that gift, like the gift of our daughter, I feel a deep gratitude to providence. Both have been a blessing, notwithstanding the natural difficulties involved in being a parent and an artist. I cannot think of anything else with which I would have chosen to fill my life.

Postscript

בָּרוּךְ אַתָּה יהוה

אֱלֹהֵינוּ מֶלֶךְ הָעוֹלָם

שֶׁהֶחֱיָנוּ וְקִיְּמָנוּ

וְהִגִּיעָנוּ לַזְּמַן הַזֶּה.

'Blessed are you Lord, our God, King of the Universe, who has given us life, sustained us and brought us to this time.' In the Jewish tradition this is said in Hebrew at significant moments of life.

I repeat it here in thanksgiving for the life I feel privileged and grateful to have received. I have been able to pursue a lifelong development through being given the gift and the love of music. Not only for my personal fulfilment was this gift but it flourished over the years and led to my aiding a younger generation in finding their way in life and music. Thus teaching as well as performing music became the central thread in my journey through life, notwithstanding its struggles and elations.

I'll reiterate here the words my great friend Dr Schossberger wrote to me at a critical moment in my life, which came to be fulfilled: 'There stood an earthenware jug at the side of the road with the inscription: I went through fire to hold water for the thirsty traveller.' That jar makes me feel humbled and grateful for all I have received and been able to pass on.

Holocaust Memorial Day Notes from School Pupils

A s one of the dwindling number of survivors of the Holocaust, I have felt it important to share my personal experience of it with the younger generation. For some years now, therefore, I have participated in Holocaust Memorial Days by speaking to secondary school pupils. In recounting the story of my Holocaust experiences to these young people of an impressionable age, I am able on each occasion to stress the tragic absurdity of prejudice and fixed ideas which can, and often do, lead to acts of violence, as it did under the Nazi regime.

These talks are always received by the young people with great attention, and spark off questions which prove that a personal account of such experience resonates with them, and relates to their own feelings. Some of their written responses have been chosen from the hundreds I have received over the years after giving such talks to teenage pupils.

HMD

I feel very sorry about how you lost your father but I have even had that experiance lossing my father.
It is very intresting to know how you survived and if I was you I would have lost hope, not like you. So you are very brave.

NAME   SCHOOL Rosedale College.

HMD

I really enjoyed listening to your experiences. Although it was heart breaking it was very intresting to hear your past. This has taught me to respect one another and that everyone is equal and hopefully our generation can learn from this.

NAME   SCHOOL Marlborough

HMD

I am truly moved and touched by your story of your child hood. I can't imagine the overflow of emotions you must have experienced during and after the war, but i am thankful of the memories you have shared. I have Jewish heritage on my fathers side and couldn't imagine losing them. I am inspired by you and your bravery, especially from such a young age.
I just want to thank you for your time and your inspirational story, thank you.

NAME   SCHOOL Queens School

Dear Nelly

Thank you so much for
Sharing your past with us today. I was
really moved by what you have said
today, and am inspired to write
about it.

I am also very interested in the ~~plano~~
piano, and music, and you have inspired
me to achieve my goals and try my
best. You are, truly, an inspiration.
Best wishes

NAME   **SCHOOL** Hockerill

Dear Nelly,

your story has moved me. you are
brave and courageous. you have taught
Me to live life to the fullest
and to not judge or discriminate
others. Thank you for your
wonderful and memorable speech.

NAME   **SCHOOL** Tring School

I enjoyed your talk
very much ☺. While happy for
you I am still saddened by what
this terrible event shows ~~what~~ how
some humans can be awful.

NAME   **SCHOOL** Watford Grammar

Dear Nelly,

I loved listening to your story. It will stay with me forever and you are a true inspiration for many. I respect what you have gone through and thank that you had the courage and strength to tell us!

NAME

SCHOOL Hockerill

Hello Nelly,

Your talk was very interesting and most importantly thought provoking. It made me realise the value and fragility of life and how we must strive to protect it. How one day later you and your mother would have died. It also showed me how kind people can be to some, while they cause death and suffering to others (the ss soldiers). I realise how lucky we are to be so safe in todays society and how we need to protect this. I would like to thank you for bravely telling your memories of the past to talk to us and thank the Lord you survived remaining were later died. Thank you Matthew.

NAME

SCHOOL Tring School

---

to Nellie,

Thank you for sharing your story with us today. It has really opened our eyes to the true horrors of the Holocaust and the damage it caused to millions of lives like your own.

thank you.

NAME

SCHOOL Hitchin boys' school

APPENDIX II

Some Memorabilia from a Musical Career

Piano Variations
MOZART BEETHOVEN SCHUBERT
MENDELSSOHN CHOPIN

Nelly Ben-Or

Mazurcas para piano
de Polonia y México
Mazurcas for piano, from Poland and Mexico
NELLY BEN-OR, PIANO

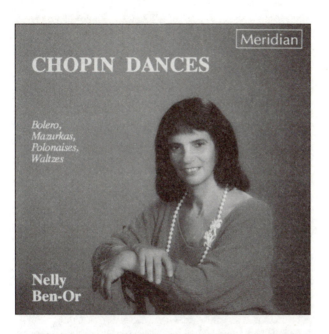

Meridian

CHOPIN DANCES

Bolero,
Mazurkas,
Polonaises,
Waltzes

Nelly
Ben-Or

DUO

FRANZ SCHUBERT
Impromptus D899 & D935

Nelly Ben-Or - piano

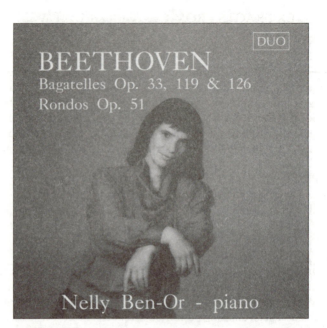

DUO

BEETHOVEN
Bagatelles Op. 33, 119 & 126
Rondos Op. 51

Nelly Ben-Or - piano

Meridian

BEETHOVEN

PIANO QUARTET IN E FLAT MAJOR, Opus 16.
SERENADE IN D MAJOR, Opus 8.

Nelly Ben-Or - Piano.
The Jerusalem String Trio.

EXTRACTS FROM CONCERT REVIEWS

LONDON
POETICAL FEELING OF POLISH-BORN PIANIST
In Chopin's Four Impromptus and the Andante Spianato &
Grande Polonaise she moulded their long phrases with artistry
using a wide range of tone colour. Miss Ben-Or played both
books of Debussy's Images with much poetical feeling, equally at
home in the flashing colours of 'Poissons d'Or' as in the nostalgic
imagery of 'Cloches à travers les feuilles'. *Daily Telegraph*

PARIS
This pianist has the real qualities of musicality, sensitivity and
intelligence. *Vlado Perlemuter*

AMSTERDAM
DISTINGUISHED PLAYING OF NELLY BEN-OR
With a particularly remarkable performance of Chopin's second
sonata the pianist showed all her great qualities. The Marche
Funebre was performed with an outstanding intensity and the Finale
received such an amazing performance as I have rarely heard.
Niewe Rotterdam Courant

BELFAST
Nelly Ben-Or has clearly amassed a formidable reputation in her
world travels. In the Schumann her fine technique was always
a means to an end and not, as so often happens, an end in itself.
These were deeply felt performances. *Belfast Telegraph*

JERUSALEM
A MAJOR PIANIST CAME TO TOWN
Nelly Ben-Or gave a recital that showed her to be a real musician
as well as a splendid performer. In the Haydn sonata she conveyed
the work's nobility, strength and inventiveness. The contrasts in
the character of Schubert's Impromptus could hardly have been
bettered. *Jerusalem Post*

SYDNEY
Her playing was full of vitality and strength, responding equally
well to the storms of Schumann and finding in Chopin a poetic
vein that was never over-exploited. *Morning Herald*

Bibliography

Alexander, F. Matthias, *Man's Supreme Inheritance* (London: Methuen & Co., 1910)

—— *Constructive Conscious Control of the Individual* (London: Methuen & Co., 1924)

—— *The Use of the Self* (London: Methuen & Co., 1931)

—— *The Universal Constant in Living* (London: Chaterson, 1942)

(The books listed above can be obtained from The Society of Teachers of the Alexander Technique (STAT))

Barlow, Wilfred, *The Alexander Principle* (London: Gollancz, 1990)

Ben-Or, Nelly, 'A Pianist's Thoughts on the Alexander Technique', *The Alexander Journal*, No. 8, Autumn 1978

—— 'A Pianist's Adventure with the Alexander Technique', *The Alexander Journal*, No. 11, Spring 1979

—— 'The Alexander Technique: Its Relevance to Performance', *Journal of the International Society for the Study of Tension in Performance*, Vol. 1, No. 1, November 1983

—— *The Alexander Technique in the Preparation and Performance of Music*

—— 'On the Alexander Technique and Performance', in Carola Grindea (ed.), *Tensions in the Performance of Music* (Amersham: Kahn & Averill, 1995)

Davies, Norman, *Rising '44: The Battle for Warsaw* (London: Macmillan, 2004)

Macdonald, Patrick, *The Alexander Technique as I See It* (London: Mouritz, 1989)

Marshall, Robert, *In the Sewers of Lvov* (London: HarperCollins, 1990)

Miller, Malcolm, 'Keeping in Line: an Interview with Nelly Ben-Or', in *Music and Musicians*, Vol. 17, No. 4, 2008

Rubinstein, Arthur, *My Many Years* (London: Jonathan Cape, 1980)

Wells, Leon, *The Janowska Road: Survival in a Nazi Death Camp* (CreateSpace Independent Publishing, 2014)

Zamoyski, Adam, *Poland: A History* (London: William Collins, 2015)

Index